Strategic Thinking in Tactical Times

Edited by

Joseph DiVanna

and

François Austin

First published 2004 by
PALGRAVE MACMILLAN
Houndmills, Basingstoke, Hampshire RG21 6XS and
175 Fifth Avenue, New York, N.Y. 10010
Companies and representatives throughout the world

PALGRAVE MACMILLAN is the global academic imprint of the Palgrave Macmillan division of St. Martin's Press, LLC and of Palgrave Macmillan Ltd. Macmillan® is a registered trademark in the United States, United Kingdom and other countries. Palgrave is a registered trademark in the European Union and other countries.

ISBN 1–4039–3406–1

This book is printed on paper suitable for recycling and made from fully managed and sustained forest sources.

A catalogue record for this book is available from the British Library.

Library of Congress Cataloging-in-Publication Data
    Strategic thinking in tactical times / edited by Joseph DiVanna and François Austin.
        p. cm.
    Includes bibliographical references and index.
    ISBN 1–4039–3406–1 (cloth)
        1. Strategic planning. I. DiVanna, Joseph A. II. Austin, François, 1966–

HD30.28.S735227 2004
658.4'012—dc22   2003063273

10 9 8 7 6 5 4 3 2 1
13 12 11 10 09 08 07 06 05 04

Printed and bound in Great Britain by
Antony Rowe Ltd, Chippenham and Eastbourne

Contents

List of Figures

Acknowledgements

First and foremost, we would like to thank all the participants in the Book-in-a-Day event held in London on 30 June–1 July, 2003. Their willingness to tackle the impossible task by taking time from their busy schedules to participate in the event was instrumental in shaping the tenor of this book. Each person's ability to place various aspects of today's changing world into the context of strategy, strategy development, the execution of strategic initiatives and finally the manifestation of tactics, provides the reader with a sense of practicality in the application of strategic thought to the process of everyday business.

The participants

Shaharazad Abuel-Ealeh – Careers Research and Advisory Council (CRAC)
Stuart Bradley – Corven
Sarah Byrne-Quinn – Cable & Wireless plc
Nick Coyle – Corven
John Dembitz – Boyden Global Executive Search
David Doyle – Prudential plc
Michael Emmerson – Leisure Media
Ray Grime – Bank of Bermuda
Dr Eric Grunwald – Perihelion
William James – LCF Rothschild Securities Limited
Kevan Jones – Corven
James Leaton-Gray – BBC
Nigel Lloyd – Cambridge Professional Development

Jeff Morgan – Computer Sciences Corporation (CSC)
Janice Nagourney – Thought Leaders International
Peter Parker – EPCot Systems
Milagros Perez-Novoa – Cambridge Entrepreneurship Centre
Jane Roe – Corven
David Shirreff – The Economist
Lauren Smith – Direct Line
Ian Southward – Fiserv CCS
Richard Tannahill – GSK
Diana Thomas – Institute of Leadership and Management
Bryan Thresher – Misys International Banking Systems
Jason Turner – Tactical Networks
Alan Whitaker – Business Futurist
Arif Zaman – British Airways

We would also like to thank our publisher Stephen Rutt at Palgrave Macmillan, for his continuous support, unending patience during the development of the manuscript and his willingness to take a risk on prototyping a new process in book development and provide strategy practitioners with a platform for their views on strategic thinking. The production of this book would not be possible without the hard work of the staff of Palgrave Macmillan: Sanphy Thomas, Jackie Kippenberger, Fionnuala Kennedy and Anna Van Boxel. A·special thanks to all the people at Corven who spent many hours in the development and preparation of the event, reading and editing the manuscript, and acting as thought partners during the production of this book. We are grateful for the extreme patience and understanding of Ian Head, at Head-e Designs, Ltd for facilitating the production of the Book-in-a-Day event under less than ideal conditions; he is the exemplar of the phrase 'necessity is the mother of invention'. Last but by no means least; we would like to thank Isabel DiVanna for her diligence in reading and re-reading the manuscript copies of this text.

Preface

About the book

The bulk of the ideas, concepts and dialogue of this book are the direct result of a two-day event in which the Corven and Maris Strategies brought together strategy practitioners of diverse backgrounds from a wide variety of firms. This book treats the participants as reference sources and refers to their thinking at the event by identifying them by last name equal to any published source. In some cases, individuals present an idea or concept that occurred at his/her company or in their past experience or makes reference to a concept, which has originated at another source, and where possible the originating reference has been identified and included for ease of reference. For example, a participant may discuss a concept used at their firm such as the balanced score card which is attributed to Kaplan and Norton. During the two-day event, the group discussed, argued and debated the issues that are challenging companies in the development strategy under adverse business conditions. The exploration of the group centred on the notion that many strategic initiatives have been jettisoned in favour of attaining short-term tactical objectives.

The idea for a 'Book in a Day' was conceived many years ago by business author Joseph DiVanna while at CSC Index, after viewing a film called *The Four-hour House* based on the 1983 competition sponsored by the Building Industry Association of San Diego County to build a house from foundation to finish while complying with strict building codes to set a world record.[1] DiVanna's original intention was to develop a mechanism for the financial institutions to rapidly devise and plan the competitive strategies for banking services. Using industry experts from banks operating in various geographies, the plan was to bring together practitioners from various parts of banking institutions to seek out common trends in the financial services industry that can be used to develop specific customer value propositions. Unfortunately, the original event was scheduled for the week following 11 September 2001 and was subsequently cancelled. It was not until earlier this year that DiVanna partnered with François Austin at the Corven Group, bringing the idea into a reality. DiVanna, a board member of the Strategic Planning Society in London and Austin the director of a venture capital and management-consulting firm used their network of business contacts to extend invitations to a collection of industry professionals with diverse skills, backgrounds and perspectives on corporate strategies. Working with DiVanna's publisher Palgrave Macmillan, 'The Book in a Day Workshop' migrated from its original theme of financial services to one that is even more appropriate to today's business climate, that of Strategy and Strategic Thinking.

The intent of the book is to provide insight into the revolution occurring in how corporations create and execute strategies. DiVanna believes that strategy development is shifting from a function traditionally restricted to an elite group within a company to a process in which strategic thinking must now aggregate across an organization's many levels into a cohesive set of strategic initiatives that are driven by sensing changes in the business environment. To make the transition successful, corporations must integrate the act of strategy development into the fabric of their business processes making them able to sense changes in the business climate and initiate tactical adjustments based on preconceived scenarios.

Armed with delegates from organizations such as CSC, Careers Research and Advisory Centre (CRAC, Cambridge), Bank of Bermuda, Misys International Banking Systems, The Royal Institute of International Affairs, Prudential, Direct Line Insurance, the Institute of Leadership and Management, amongst many others, and several senior members of the Strategic Planning Society, the event took place in a semi-sequestered environment at the Le Meriden Hotel in Piccadilly, London. Nineteen delegates, four facilitators, two graphic artists and six event coordinators gathered to do what seemed to be impossible: write a bulk of book on modern strategy in 24 hours. How could this be possible?

The event was designed around a simple premise, if you assemble smart people and give them a seemingly impossible task, they will pull together and produce breakthrough ideas. DiVanna and Austin devised a methodology that uses the construction of a book with subchapters as a means to discuss, explore and create a dialogue along a predetermined agenda, resembling a table of contents. The starting point was a series of short lectures explaining the objective of the workshop, the predefined structure of the book to be written, the content of the chapters and several aspects of strategy and strategic thinking in today's business environment. Next, the delegates were presented with a series of nine 15-minute lectures featuring speakers from industry and academia portraying a wide variety of views on strategic thinking. Immediately after the lectures, attendees were challenged with a team-building exercise to break the ice and demonstrate the value of having a business vision. Following a working lunch, three teams were formed in specially designed working areas, one for each chapter of the book-to-be. Engaging in a process of formal and informal discussion sessions, attendees separated themselves in three groups, each focusing on a specific chapter and issues entering into impassioned debates about various facets of developing corporate strategies. Ninety minutes later, delegates regrouped and began producing written components of content. As delegates wrote on flipcharts and paper, the graphics and text produced by all three groups were converted into PowerPoint presentations and Microsoft Word documents by graphic artists who were resident in the room. The process of the book's development is illustrated in Figure 0.1.

After what everyone considered a very short 120 minutes, participants rotated to a different work area and refocused themselves debating another chapter and a new set of topics. The idea was to give every attendee a chance to debate on every single sub-chapter of the book. The process was repeated a third time, and after the exhausting brainstorming session, dinner was served. In the last group debate, participants were informed that they were expected to select three subchapters, write approximately 400 words on each subtopic over night, and bring their contributions to the graphics people by the next morning. A number of delegates stayed in their working areas until 9:30 pm, 13 hours after the strategy seminar had started! Upon completing this task each delegate could either keep working to expand on their issues further developing the topics, or start working on a completely different

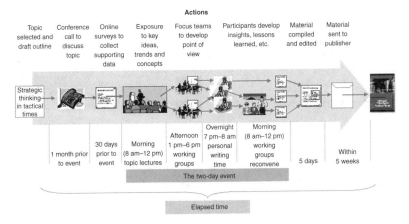

Figure 0.1 The Book-in-a-Day process

chapter or sub-chapter. The graphic artists and support staff worked into the night to record all the activities of the day for review the next morning.

Tuesday brought an early start – 45 per cent of the attendees were on their tables writing by 8:00 am, a half-hour before the scheduled start. The entire morning was a frantic race against the clock, as time was the common enemy. As soon as attendees produced text or graphics in writing, the graphic artist and content coordinators typed and shaped their contribution directly into the book. A gigantic chart was maintained to coordinate the activities of each delegate and progress towards the intended goals. The word count was impressive: by 12 noon on day two, we had 9000 words; by 1 pm we had 17 000 words, by 2 pm we had 24 000 words and by the time the last attendee begged for mercy, at 4 pm, we had 29 000 words. Some delegates chose to email their contribution so by 6 pm on day two the team achieved a total of 75 graphics and 34 700 words!

The delegates spent two days debating, discussing, writing, team building and networking. By the end of the event, they had all survived the unusual working conditions with almost half the delegates expressing an interest in participating in a similar workshop in the future. The feedback session was very positive, with a number of insightful improvements being suggested to improve the productivity of the process that will be incorporated into the design of future workshops. During the remainder of the month of July and early August 2003, the materials generated for the book were edited by Joseph DiVanna, of Maris Strategies Limited, and François Austin of Corven.

The attendees' feedback

What worked

Attendees seem to think that the lectures in the morning session were useful and provided valuable insight. Most delegates would have preferred to have more freedom as far as working groups went, but they all agreed that without structure they probably would not have been as productive in a captive environment. Attendees agreed that being in one group in day one and moving around, as a group, between the chapters of the book, enabled them to get to work well with each other. The day two activities with specially designed for written-production time was also helpful as it allowed new thinking to emerge. They all agreed that the variety of voices were very useful, as a narrowly focused debate would have limited the possibilities for discussion and new output. Being residential at the hotel was also seen as a positive element of the experience, as late night bar conversations helped them unwind and yet focus (although the graphics artists did not agree that doodles from the bar conversations were all that helpful or easy to make into PowerPoint presentations). Overall, all participants who stayed for the feedback considered that this was a good experience, and more than half of them said that they looked forward to the next event.

What could be improved

A few delegates said that by the end of day one, they were very unclear on where the event was going; one delegate suggested that it was because no one knew what the others were producing. Delegates suggested having a tape recorder or a microphone and recorded on the tables, as so many discussions were not recorded in writing and therefore lost. A few said that the morning session was too long and led attendees to believe that this was just another workshop where people deliver lectures and others are put to produce very little compared to their intellectual capacity. Lectures would have been better appreciated if spread along the two days. Attendees also suggested that on day two, people working on the same chapters could be put together for more collaborative writing. They thought that day two lacked dialogue and interaction as they were 'too free' to move around and chat and discuss with whoever was in the room. A few delegates found that the chapter headings constrained the conversation/thinking. Although participants said that they felt they lacked freedom, in the end they all agreed that no framework would not have worked. Attendees also said that perhaps a brainstorm process/private writing followed by presentation of content would have been better. Delegates also thought that although they felt ownership for each case study individually, they did not have and would not have ownership of the whole book. Some of them also warned that prior permission for case studies would be useful, and more teams for the team-building activities would have helped to build team spirit. Although the premise of the workshop was to write a book in 24 hours, some delegates said that they needed time to challenge thinking and text the work.

Final note

The comments and feedback from delegates seemed to cover two issues: lack of freedom and too much freedom. Where they lacked freedom (day one), they felt that this was to an extent harmful to their intellectual and creative capacity. Where they had too much freedom (day two), they felt that it was detrimental to dialogue and interaction. One thing to be learned is that the balance between having a task and having to complete it and completing the task as one wishes is hard to find. It will be immensely helpful to consider these points for future workshops with similar aims.

Notes on Contributors

Attendees

Alan Whitaker

As an internationally respected keynote speaker, future trends analyst, strategic planning facilitator and trainer, Alan has made presentations attended by more than 150 000 chief executives, directors, managers and specialists. His clients regard him as a leading futurist, thinker and exponent of strategic planning. Using his facilitation skills, many of his clients have reinvented and re-energized their organizations to become leaders in their industry. A self-made man, after the death of his father he completed the last two years of his schooling and two university degrees by part-time study. Before setting up his own consultancy in 1978, he held senior positions in the food and transport industries. He lives in London but speaks and consults around the world. He is a Fellow of the Institute of Directors.

Bryan Thresher

Bryan is Solutions Marketing Manager for Misys Retail Banking. He has worked for a UK high street bank and several leading IT suppliers in the retail banking industry. Before joining Misys, he was an independent consultant in leading edge retail banking technology, specializing in custom market research for the major players in the market. He speaks at international retail banking conferences, and regularly gives briefings on key issues relating to retail banking.

David Doyle

David joined Prudential plc in September 1996. He was promoted to Head of Corporate Finance in 2000, where he has responsibility for the group's merger and acquisitions activities. He has led and been involved in numerous merger, acquisition and divestment assignments including

the acquisition of M&G, the proposed merger with American General and the disposal of the Group's UK general insurance and German life insurance businesses. Prior to Prudential, David spent 10 years with Arthur Andersen. David is a Fellow of the Institute of Chartered Accountants in Australia and holds a Bachelor of Business degree from the Royal Melbourne Institute of Technology. Away from the office, David is a keen skier, a cricket romantic and a poor but persistent golfer. He enjoys all forms of travel, but particularly when it involves discovering great food and wine.

David Shirreff

Since 2001, David has been capital markets editor for *The Economist*. From September 2003, he will be finance and business correspondent in Frankfurt. David worked from September 2000 to March 2001 as a financial zone editor for *Net Profit Publications*, a publishing and consulting company which specializes in eCommerce. David was the Managing Editor of the *Euromoney magazine* and worked as a freelance financial journalist for *Risk*, *International Media Partners*, *Global Finance*, *Investment Dealers' Digest* and *The Wall Street Journal*. David previously worked as a journalist in Turkey (for Reuters), and as a teacher of English in Germany and Turkey. He has a degree in English from Oriel College, Oxford and is interested in fine art, theatre, skiing, running and wine.

Diana Thomas

Freelance writer, editor and publisher and currently Managing Editor of the journals of the Institute of Leadership and Management. Previously Head of Open Learning at Newcastle Business School, University of Northumbria. She has managed the development and production of a range of mixed media management development series and acted as consultant on learning strategy and presentation of specialist information for non-specialist readerships for, amongst others, The King's Fund, Open University, Butterworth Heinemann and the Health Education Council.

Eric Grunwald

Eric runs Perihelion, a company dedicated to helping businesses understand how their environment might develop and how to use this understanding to plot a course into the future. His previous experience was with ICI and Shell, where he worked for six years in the Far East and also in the scenario group in London, and with BUPA, where he was a Group Strategy and Development Director. His forthcoming book *Double Vision* deals with how two very different worldviews illuminate many of the problems we face today and how these different points of view are also reflected in science, mathematics, language, economics and mythology. His second book takes some of these themes further.

François Austin

François Austin is a Founding Director of Corven. With more than 12 years of consultancy experience, François Austin has focused on translating business strategies and ideas into demonstrable commercial results. He specializes in the areas of strategy, post merger integration, innovation and driving performance within existing business units. François has worked in the United States, Asia and Europe, equipping him with a deep perspective and understanding of the challenges that face global organizations. François has also contributed to the best-selling management books *The Discipline of Market Leaders* (Michael Treacy, Fred Wiersema) and *Surfing on the Edge of Chaos* (Richard Pascale, Mark Millemann, Linda Gioja).

Ian Southward

Ian Southward has over 20 years experience in banking and IT. He has held a variety of management positions in sales, marketing, project management and consultancy for leading companies such as TSB Bank,

Unisys and Tandem Computers. He has run his own consultancy practice and now is Managing Director of a CRM software and services business in the United Kingdom. Ian is a trained banker who has considerable experience in the many areas of technology applications in banking. Ian is a regular seminar speaker and has authored various published articles for the Institute of Financial Services, covering topics such as distribution channels, eCommerce, customer relationship management, data warehousing and m-commerce.

James Leaton-Gray

James Leaton-Gray has been working in broadcasting, mainly for the BBC, for over 25 years. Much of his time as a programme maker was spent in political journalism; he edited many of the BBC's Political and Parliamentary programmes including Today/Yesterday in Parliament, The Week in Westminster, Westminster Live and the documentary series, Scrutiny. He is now the Executive, Editorial Projects at the BBC, in which role he oversees a wide range of management tasks. He was one of the first staff members to be invited to take part in the BBC MBA programme. He is a trustee of the Strategic Planning Society and Chairman of its TMT group. He is also a member of the Chartered Management Institute.

Jason Turner

Jason Turner is an expert in operational risk management. He is applying highly sophisticated database driven techniques to increase the organizational resilience of large organizations. He is currently employed by Tactical Networks, where he has been developing sophisticated systems for the banking industry. Turner advocates the use of technology to comprehensively coordinate the formulation and implementation of strategies and tactics.

Jeff Morgan

Jeff Morgan is a Managing Consultant with Computer Sciences Corporation (CSC) and he has nearly 40 years experience in IT and business, 30 years of which has been in management consulting and project management, in retail, manufacturing, government and public sector organizations. His assignments range from business strategy and feasibility studies through to project and contract assessment; he has managed small projects and teams in large projects and has practical experience of systems integration. In the last few years he has worked extensively in programme management for business change, and in knowledge management. Jeff's first-hand experience has provided an insight into what works well and what works less well in strategy implementation.

Joseph DiVanna

Joseph DiVanna is an independent author, consultant and global public speaker based in Cambridge, England where he researches the nature and behaviour of business during the last 10 centuries. His lectures have prompted many attendees to develop new interests in the study of medieval history, commerce and technology. A thought leader and a re-engineering practitioner formerly with CSC Index's Research and Advisory Services, he is currently the CEO of Maris Strategies, Ltd where he has authored four books, *Redefining Financial Services: the New Renaissance in Value Propositions, Thinking beyond Technology, Creating New Value in Business, Synconomy: Adding Value in a World of Continuously Connected Business* and *The Future of Retail Banking* all published by Palgrave Macmillan. As a leisure activity he directs the research on the medieval construction of King's College Chapel, Cambridge.

John Dembitz

After graduating with an MBA from London Business School, John Dembitz spent five years as a Consultant with McKinsey & Co.; he then became an Executive Director of Amey Roadstone responsible for strategy; following which he joined Charterhouse, an investment bank,

becoming an Executive Director, Corporate Finance. In 1985 he was appointed CEO of Valin Pollen, then the United Kingdom's largest and fastest growing corporate and financial communications consultancy. He subsequently spent five years as COO and part owner of IDOM SA, an IT consultancy with offices throughout Central and Eastern Europe, before it was sold to Deloitte & Touche. Today he is the Chairman of three companies, a Non-executive Director, and has two businesses of his own, as well as being on the Regional Advisory Board of London Business School.

Lauren Smith

Lauren's current role is Strategic Development Manager for Direct Line's Retail Division. One of Lauren's main challenges is to ensure future thinking and Scenario Planning pulled into a robust Strategic Planning process. After graduating from the University of Bristol in 1999, she spent a year at the Cooperative Insurance Society in Manchester where she encountered the traditional practices and values held by one of the more traditional members of the Insurance Industry. This insight proves invaluable to her at Direct Line everyday, striving to be at the opposite end of the industry spectrum in everything we do.

Milagros Perez-Novoa

Milagros Perez-Novoa has over 10 years experience as a Corporate Financier. Before joining the Cambridge MBA in 2001, Milagros was a Financial Manager in Corporate Finance at Banca Commerciale Italiana (Intesa Group). Before that, she was part of the Corporate Banking team at BankBoston. Other roles have included undertaking equity research in the portfolio and risk management of the Lima Stock Exchange and forming part of the financial advisory team to the Peruvian Government for the privatization of the telecom and mining companies in association with Deutsche Bank and

PriceWaterhouseCoopers. After her MBA, Milagros joined as an Associate to Cambridge Investment Research Ltd. Milagros also has been a Consultant to Clerical Medical, the asset management arm of the Halifax Bank of Scotland. Now she is working as an Economic Researcher for the Cambridge MIT Institute and as a consultant on Investment Management to CFS Partners Ltd, a London-based investment bank.

Nigel Lloyd

Nigel Lloyd is the Principal of Cambridge Professional Development www.CamProf.com, the consultancy he founded in 1994. CamProf works across Europe and has expertise in specifying the competences of professionals and developing business applications for competences (including career management, continuing professional development, assessment, training, recruitment and selection). Together with four other consultancies, CamProf has set up 5S Consulting Ltd, www.5sconsulting.com with offices across the United Kingdom. Nigel is a Chartered Civil Engineer and Fellow of the Chartered Institute of Personnel & Development. He spent much of his career working in Africa, SE Asia and the Indian Subcontinent. In his spare time, Nigel rows and coxes on the river Cam, and explores Europe.

Peter Parker

Peter Parker is the Managing Director of EPCoT Systems Ltd. After a degree and postgraduate work in psychology, Peter moved into the IT world. He has successfully worked in companies that built much of the Middle East infrastructure before working for a major mini computer manufacturer in International Sales Support. In 1978, Peter set up EPCoT Systems Ltd and under his guidance the company has expanded and provides services to retail, financial and government related organizations. In recent years the delivery of EPCoT Systems has been recognized by two awards from Deloitte and Touche. Peter was recently seconded to HFEA as an interim to steer the IT and systems side of the organization to a more secure base. Peter's main background is in the understanding of process, and EPCoT has its own process delivery software solutions.

Ray Grime

Ray Grime is 54 years old. Ray is married with three grown-up daughters. He is currently working as a Senior Project Manager for Bank of Bermuda, one of the largest Fund Managers. Has spent virtually all his career working on IT related projects. Ray spent 22 years at a Systems House, which have varied from Defence related to Market Making to Weather Forecasting.

Richard Tannahill

Richard Tannahill joined GlaxoSmithKline in March 1989 as Director, Corporate Audit, where he led a team providing an internal consulting service. In 1993, he assumed responsibility for developing SmithKline Beecham's Finance 10 > 3/1 (strategic) plan, as well as the development and implementation of the company's 3/1 (operational) planning process. In 1996, he moved to The Netherlands as Finance Director and is currently Finance Director of Consumer Healthcare R&D.

Shaharazad Abuel-Ealeh

Shaharazad Abuel-Ealeh joined Careers Research and Advisory Council (CRAC) in 2002, working on CRAC's work-related learning programme for school and HE students, InsightPlus™. Since then, she has taken on responsibility for a collaborative European research programme, a national awards scheme for volunteering and additional communications functions. Previously, Shaharazad was an Account Manager for Making Waves Communications (2000–02), where she was responsible for creating, planning, budgeting and managing youth/student campaigns. From 1998–2000, she was an elected officer of the University of Warwick Students' Union. Shaharazad's first role was Student Activities Officer, where she was responsible for running and consolidating the organization's non-commercial strategic planning process. She continued this in her second role, Communications Officer, working towards the overall planning for the organization.

Facilitators

Jane Roe

Jane Roe is a consultant with Corven responsible for the delivery of consulting projects. Whilst at Corven, Jane has worked with clients across industries looking at both strategy development as well as operational performance improvement. Prior to Corven, Jane was a Senior Consultant at Mitchell Madison Group and worked on a range of strategy consulting projects including internet strategy, marketing strategy, pricing strategy and performance improvement mainly in financial services, entertainment and not-for-profit sectors. Jane has an MBA from INSEAD. She also has a Masters degree in Chemistry and is a Doctorate in Organic Chemistry, both from Oxford.

Kevan Jones

Kevan Jones is a Founding Director of Corven accountable for major consulting assignments. He has more than 15 years of consulting experience where he has focused on translating business strategies and ideas into demonstrable commercial results. This work has covered everything from major transformational projects through to establishing new ventures in a diverse range of industries across different cultures and continents – Europe, Asia and South America. Prior to Corven, Kevan was an independent consultant for two years working with an international network of clients in Europe and the United States. Prior to this, he worked for five years with CSC Index.

Nick Coyle

Nick Coyle is a consultant with Corven. With over 17 years of experience in consulting and general management, he has successfully led and

delivered various projects through strategy, planning and implementation. Nick has worked with major organizations across Europe, North America and South East Asia. Nick has a BSc. in Business Economics from the University of Wales, Cardiff, an MBA from the School of Management, Bradford and an MSc. in Information Management from The Management School, Lancaster University.

Stuart Bradley

Stuart Bradley is a consultant with Corven, and has delivered projects for clients in Finance, Telecommunications and Electricity sectors. His experience includes management of process change programmes, and management of Labs and Work-Out™ programmes, focusing on the alignment of strategic cultural shift, innovation and operational enhancement. Prior to Corven, Stuart was a Senior Strategy Consultant with Gemini Consulting (now CGE&Y) and worked on a range of strategy and operations projects within the chemicals, utilities, steel and travel sectors, in the United Kingdom and Europe. Stuart has Bachelor and Doctorate degrees in Chemical Engineering from Swansea and Cambridge Universities, and has an MBA from London Business School.

Technical people and coordinators

Ian Head

Ian Head is the founder and Managing Director of Head-E Design Limited and Creative and Technical Director of Bluefin Group. Ian has a traditional design background with 14 years experience, during which he has broadened his skills across a range of visual and technological disciplines. He has built up his own design business, Head-E Design, providing creative design, web-based and IT solutions for SMEs whilst concentrating on larger, long-term strategic projects with Bluefin Group. Ian has worked on the creation and production of brand identity, marketing collateral, print advertising, corporate stationery, website builds, intranet development, eCommerce solutions and other IT-related design work. Ian also loves to spend time with his family, kayak down the occasional river, learn to sail and study astronomy.

Isabel DiVanna

Isabel DiVanna graduated from the Pontifical Catholic University in 1999, after doing a BA in History and Didactics and specializing in late medieval literature. Isabel is currently living in Cambridge, England and is about to finish her PhD degree from the University of Manchester on the topic of nineteenth-century French Medievalism. Isabel was part of the event management team at the Catholic University of Rio de Janeiro (1996–99), and today she works at Maris Strategies Limited as a Finance Director. In her spare time, she helps edit Joe's books and does a lot of gardening.

Joanna Longley

Joanna Longley is responsible for the day-to-day running of the Corven office and supports the consulting team to ensure the smooth running of projects. In addition she is responsible for managing the graphics capability and organizes IT within Corven as well as community events. Joanna has a background in Graphics and managing Corporate Identity. Prior to joining Corven, she worked for Genesis Oil & Gas Consultants Ltd as Management Support, as well as dealing with corporate events and general office management.

Kate Adey

Kate Adey is a consultant with Corven, and is responsible for the Leadership Development Service Capability and the building of a network of executive coaches. Whilst specialising on client coaching assignments, Kate also delivers projects in the areas of Performance Improvement and large-scale transformation accross a variety of industries. Prior to joining

Corven, Kate worked in the Global Customer Relationship Management (CRM) business specializing in helping businesses to manage change within customer Racing environments. Kate graduated in Psychology (BSc. Hons) from St. Andrews University in 1992. She is an IHD accredited coach and facilitator and is a member of the International Coaching Federation.

Pamela Daruwalla

Pamela Daruwalla joined Corven in 2002. Her role covers HR, finance and compliance, working closely with the finance Director and accountant to manage cash flow. Pamela graduated from UCL with BA Hons Italian in 2000, which included a year at Politecnico di Milano. During University, Pamela was involved with the development of Intelligent Space, a spatial analysis consultancy and on graduating stuck with start ups and joined globalCOAL, an electronic platform enabling physical and financial trading of coal. Pamela is currently studying for a Masters in Personnel and Development, specializing in coaching.

Susan Oldman

Susan is Corven's Marketing Manager, responsible for all aspects of the Marketing Spectrum including PR, events, web presence and internal communications. Prior to Corven, Susan worked at PricewaterhouseCoopers in their Transaction Services business, as a Marketing and Client Services Assistant. Susan has a degree in Geography and Management Studies from Leeds University, where, she specialized in marketing, and is currently studying for her Postgraduate Diploma in Marketing at London Guildhall University.

The book also received contributions from Sarah Byrne-Quinn, William Jones and Michael Emmerson.

1
Introduction

Academics have argued that the relative rate of change resulting from technology and other social phenomena has not substantially increased over the years recognizing a measurable lag between a technical innovation and its practical application. Yet, business professionals and industry practitioners continue to insist that the intensity of business and the nature of competition are moving at greater and greater speeds. This dichotomy in the perception of business raises the question: how can the academics who measure the macro/micro levels of productivity and rate of business activity be right while the people in the industry hold an opinion on the rate of business that seems contrary to academic quantitative measurements? Simply, how can both groups be right? On the other hand, must one be right and the other wrong?

Three things are becoming clear in the early years of the twenty-first century: first that the rate of the emerging business change is influenced by many factors such as the speed at which technology is absorbed into the popular culture (or found useful by members of a society), second, the rate in which technology is adapted by business to improve the performance of the firm often lags behind due to the inertia of pre-existing bureaucracies, and third, the perception of value in the goods and services, produced as a result of technology or by the technology itself, is taking place in ever widening social and cultural groups in a global marketplace. One key observation is that technology has initiated a fundamental switch in business activities whereby companies, regardless of size, can now engage in global commerce less expensively than previous generations of business. The result of the continued evolution of technology and other contributing factors such as education, cultures, cyclical demands, consumer preference, political and social unrest contribute to the economic zeniths and nadirs. These converging forces are creating business conditions in which traditional approaches to developing and executing corporate strategy are no longer valid or at least invalid in their application to the changing business environment. Complicating this environment is the rising need for corporations to become more flexible in their approach to business activities. The demand for flexibility has initiated a fundamental change within companies themselves as the traditional command and control organizational hierarchies, which have been evolving over past decades are now giving way to two more holistic organizational structures; a matrix of business capabilities – such as in a consulting company – and that of a network of value in which the resources of the firm both internal and external are organized as a confederation of cells of competencies.

However, the changing rate of business does not negate the need for strategy development nor does it absolve companies from the need to act, think and perform in accordance with a strategic line of thought. These conditions nevertheless herald the need to rethink fundamentally our approach to strategy formulation along with our methods of strategy execution within the firm. Planning and strategy have a long history according to Mintzberg who notes that the history of strategic planning can be traced back to 400 BC with China's Sun Tzu and more recently to the writings of Henri Fayol, who in 1916 described having ten-yearly forecasts, revised every five years.[2] Mintzberg makes an important distinction in the preconceived notions of strategic planning within organizations by defining five key terms which are used throughout the business community; planning is future thinking, planning is controlling the future, planning is decision making, planning is integrated decision making and planning is a formalized procedure to produce an articulated result, in the form of an integrated system.[3] Mintzberg points out the irony in the situation where strategic planning finds its practice comfortably at both ends of a cultural spectrum bordered on the one end by the command-and-control economies of communist nation states and the other by the free enterprise economies of western business. One can argue that regardless of where it is practised, the process of strategy development is a valuable corporate asset. Today that process is undergoing a transformation as a business discipline moving away from an activity confined to an elite group within the firm to a process in which the strategic thinking of all members of the firm must be aggregated into a cohesive yet dynamic means of taking action based on the combined business intelligence of the firm. This redefinition of strategy development signifies that business strategy must originate within the firm from individuals closest to the transactions, interactions and relationships. Simply, strategy must become a representation of the business operating in a future state reflecting how a business will engage its customers and suppliers differently than its competitors. Two things are clear on the competitive global business landscape; strategies are no longer a luxury reserved for large companies, and strategy can no longer afford to be the product of an insulated group of strategist within the firm. The new composition of the company's resources, which are increasingly owned less and less by the firm brings forth another dilemma in the formulation of business strategy: strategy must now be inclusive of partners in a network of value while remaining exclusive in guarding competitive capabilities.

This book divides the topics of strategy development and execution in this new business climate into three intermixed perspectives. Each perspective reflects the views of the *concours* of practitioners who collaborated in the development of this book, which reports on how individuals are embracing strategic thinking in new ways to remain competitive. The practitioners also address how the business must alter its approach to initiating strategic intentions by defining new processes to aggregate business intelligence across the organization while simultaneously incorporating strategic thinking into the fabric of the organization's collective mindset. In addition, the book discusses how strategic initiatives must result in measurable tactical actions that both fulfil the intent of a strategic initiative or show progress towards its objectives, while at the same time provide intelligence in which to formulate future strategies.

Chapter 2 looks at strategy by first addressing the fundamentals of strategy development from the vantage point of an individual engaged in the process of strategy development, which we will refer to as the practitioner. Practitioners are often asked what is strategy and how is it developed? The discussion in this chapter centres on our most primal of concerns as strategic thinkers, how do the changes occurring in the business environment affect an individual within the firm, and to what degree must an individual's behaviour change to remain a valued asset to the company.

The central theme of Chapter 3 is the necessity for corporations engaged in global competition to develop internal processes that engages people throughout the organization in dialogue of strategic thinking. To make strategy development more dynamic in nature, corporations must develop sensing mechanisms that act as feedback loops feeding successive versions of their strategies. The chapter argues that strategic development itself must be adaptable with the ability to adjust to changes in business conditions as they occur. This is not to say that all changes in business conditions result in a redefinition of strategy; it does, however, indicate that any new change in business conditions must now be ranked according to its relative value or impact to the strategic activities already underway. Put simply, strategy must sense and react according to a planned set of predetermined tactical responses.

Engaging business in dynamic strategy execution is the subject of Chapter 4, which argues that today's strategies must anticipate future possibilities within a framework of tactical activities designed to alter the inherent behaviour of the customer and subsequent actions of the firm. The change in the underlying nature of strategy formation and the increasing need to demonstrate results of corporate initiatives under ever shortening timetables does not negate the need for organizations to develop strategy in favour of adopting a purely tactical and reactive approach to business. The new conditions demand that companies not only adopt new methods of strategy development but also that individuals at all levels within the organization must extend fundamental and advanced strategic thinking skills.

The intent of this book is to provide insight on the changing climate of business and prepare the reader and his/her company for new levels of competition by exposing him/her to new ideas and approaches that will in turn improve his/her ability to engage in a process that we will label enabling strategic agility. To make the corporation more competitive through strategy development and execution, individuals at all levels of the firm must develop and hone new sets of strategic thinking skills. The fundamental component to strategy development that most firms overlook is the fact that people are the most valuable strategic asset and must be fully engaged in the strategy process. The human capital of the company has an uncanny ability to formulate strategies dynamically and to execute tactical actions in a continuously changing business environment. This adaptive process is the key to a firm's long-term viability. The recognition of an individual's inherent ability to embrace strategic thinking and alter the resources of the firm to make it more competitive is the subject to which we now turn.

2
The Strategic Individual

Businesses often refer to strategy using military metaphors equating competition to a battle between rival companies. The *Oxford Advance Learners Dictionary* defines strategy as 'The art of planning and directing an operation in a war or campaign'.[4] Two things are notably absent from the formal definition: customers and employees. Ironically, the development and execution of strategy rest on these two essential ingredients in the value proposition of most companies. Customers that in military analogies appear as civilian casualties are often the targets of strategic intentions or are the indirect recipients of strategic actions. Regardless of the type of analogy to describe strategy, all strategies have three things in common: goals and objectives to be achieved, policies that guide or limit actions and a sequence of actions to accomplish the goals within the given limits or parameters.[5] In today's business climate, strategy itself is rapidly becoming a confused term as a search on the Internet finds many words associated with strategy such as Internet strategy, eCommerce strategy, brand strategy, competitive strategy, market strategy, intelligent strategy, commercial strategy and many other types of strategies. The common thread that binds all these strategies is the fact that they in turn formulate a future state, goal or condition, as observed by Nigel Lloyd from Cambridge Professional Development:

> Strategy is thinking about the future beyond simple extrapolation of the present. It allows us to try to shape the future, and to shape ourselves to cope better with the future. It is about deciding on how we expect the trends to develop and where we will try to go ourselves. It is about preparing ourselves and placing ourselves, so that we survive and prosper.

However, when we think of an organization developing a strategy the image that appears is typically that of a large organization employing strategists to devise complex competitive plans. Lloyd reminds us that strategy is not a luxury that is reserved for large firms; strategy development and more specifically strategic thinking skills must be a part of all corporations regardless of size:

> Strategic thinking is not only relevant to large corporate organizations (whether shareholder owned, or government, or charitable not for profit, for example), but also to small and micro-businesses and the self-employed. Perhaps most importantly, strategic thinking also applies to planning and shaping our individual, personal, private and family lives, as well as our working lives. Not only is there benefit for complex multinationals in coordinating their responses and ensuring the parts of an organization work together rather than negating each other, but there is advantage in attempting to place ourselves and those we love so as to be able to cope with the unknown future. We [at Cambridge Professional Development] have therefore tried to provide case studies and examples that illustrate this breadth of relevance. This has not been easy: we found we had a wealth of examples drawn from the behaviour of publicly known companies, but we were less practised at assembling examples from managing our own careers, or from very different national or organizational cultures. But strategy gains resilience by drawing on diversity, and we have tried to provide a colourful variety of case studies, so that readers from the hugely different contexts to be found on our globe, can identify with some and see the relevance of all.

Lloyd makes an important distinction between the strategy formulation practised by corporations and strategic thinking which inherently resides in everyone. Although individuals often do not realize they are practising strategy every day, the process Lloyd observes suggests that everyone in an organization possesses the fundamental understanding needed for strategy formulation. What most people lack is a formalized discipline in which to develop specific strategies. Here again, Lloyd makes a key point that the development of corporate strategies is a dynamic process which must be continually interpreted by individuals who sense changes in the business conditions by observing trends and other phenomenon and assessing their relevance to the strategic intent:

> Strategy is about interpreting general trends, developing capabilities in generic areas and taking action. The benefits of strategy come

from generating a distinction that sets the company apart from other firms: recognising a problem before others and moving to distance ourselves from the risks and costs. Identifying and qualifying opportunities as they appear, so an organization can recognise it as one of the missing pieces in their value proposition, while competitors see it as 'noise' (random background variation of no significance) to be ignored, or as a problem that should be avoided or removed. There is comfort in moving as a flock, there is benefit from sharing the accumulated wisdom of the herd, and danger in flouting it. But advantage comes from occupying a niche which is uncontested, developing a capability that has no equal, avoiding a danger which has not been generally recognised in time.

Lloyd's point is that the direction of the firm is set by strategic initiatives, which act to move the organization's value proposition in the direction or opportunities that will ultimately set it apart from other similar firms. To gain momentum towards a set of corporate objectives, an organization must first identify market opportunities and then harness the resources of the firm to capitalize on specific opportunities by setting itself apart from the competition. Realigning the resources of the firm is not a simple task often requiring management teams to create catalytic conditions within the organization to motivate people within the firm to accept the new challenge. To build on Lloyd's point, Jeff Morgan, of Computer Services Corporation (CSC), reminds us that the nature of strategic thinking begins with motivation, in which the vision of a future operating state of the firm must be conveyed by top management as the spark igniting the strategic thinking process:

What motivates a strategy? Is the birth of a strategy as simple as something like one or more senior executives voicing:

- Why aren't we the best?
- What do our competitors do that we don't?
- See what our competitors are doing? We have to face up to that!
- Why are we doing so badly with our assets compared to others?
- Why don't we become a different kind of business?
- Or maybe, let's get back to basics!
- Okay, we screwed up. What's going on?

This driving force in Morgan's opinion – the need to leave the present – is half the motivation. The key role for top management is to convey the vision and motivate the organization towards its realization; they do not have to be the originators of the vision, although in many cases they are; they must however be the champions of the vision. In Gunneson's words: 'A vision should be the result of a disciplined consensus-building process that links individual objectives and organizational objectives and builds commitment to a shared purpose.'[6] The other half is a vision of the future, to determine the direction and pace of the change. Evidence of this can be found by examining the intent behind an organization's mission statement such as the US Internal Revenue Service (IRS): '[...] to provide America's taxpayers top quality service by helping them understand and meet their tax responsibilities and by applying the tax law with integrity and fairness to all'.[7]

The strategic intention of the IRS is to provide 'top quality service to each taxpayer' which is made actionable by the tactical actions of the organization such as:

- making tax filing easier,
- provide quality tax return or account service to each taxpayer needing help,
- prompt professional and helpful treatment to taxpayers in cases where additional taxes may be due,
- increase fairness of compliance,
- higher productivity through a quality work environment,
- increase employee job satisfaction.

Morgan points out that the heart of the IRS strategy is neither in the functions the organization provides nor in the tactical actions taken by the organization in response to the taxpayer or new tax legislation but in the organization's stated principles: 'The IRS will approach and solve problems from the taxpayers point of view.' To develop this customer-(taxpayer)-centric value proposition the IRS must think like a taxpayer. Fortunately, the employees of the IRS are taxpayers and can readily use their own experiential knowledge of tax filings and service as a baseline in the development of their strategy and subsequent tactical actions. Unfortunately, from a business perspective most organizations provide services to customers whose detailed business activities are foreign to employees of the firm providing the services. This does not mean that every individual in the firm must be versed in the idiosyncrasies of each customer's business. However, it does imply that individuals within the corporation must possess a skill set capable of placing each customer's need into a context of which fulfilling the need aligns with both long-term strategic objectives and shorter-term tactical goals.

Therefore, it is imperative that each individual within the firm develops a clear understanding of the company's expressed goals. More importantly, the individual must recognize how he/she can acquire skills to enable them to actively assess and improve the company's value proposition. Alan Whittaker provides us with statistics that reveal that possessing the skills for strategic thinking is only part of the solution, and that communicating strategic initiatives to members of the firm is also a key activity.

> Less than 10% of strategies are implemented and only 5% of workforce understands strategy. This begs the questions: What is the purpose of a strategy? Should strategy be implemented as conceived or does it act like a personal ambition, a pulling force describing a future that will be implemented in some form? Firms must ask themselves an even more fundamental question: once presented with it, do people tasked with implementation understand the strategy?

Whittaker raises several important questions underscoring the basic fact that without a consistently communicated and clearly understood vision delineated by defined strategic objectives, even the best strategies fall victim to poor execution and fail to initiate a process in which tactical manoeuvres can be used to take corrective action. It is in this context that individuals must act as the 'bridge' between strategy and tactical execution.

The key to becoming a strategic individual is to develop a perspective that is broad, encompassing many factors while understanding the relativity of the broader view to the specific business unit and corporate objectives. Individuals with a strategic mindset simply understand how to interpret external factors and their influence on internal goals and objectives of the firm.

We concur with Lloyd, Morgan and Whittaker in their assessment of strategy being more than simple process within the firm; strategy is a corporate competency, which now must be formed by a process of aggregating the strategic thinking capabilities of individuals across the firm channelling resources towards long- and short-term objectives. To move from strategy to tactical actions, strategic initiatives must be formatted in a way understandable by the entire organization. The individual sits at the epicentre of the new process of strategy development because of the firm's intrinsic need to sense business condition and react accordingly. Individuals with strategic thinking skills in turn execute tactical actions that are bounded by the strategic objectives. In most cases this strategic-tactical arbitrage is performed by the same individuals, who are responsible for the implementation.

However, as Mintzberg points out, since the 1960s ten schools of strategic thought have come about with the emergence of the concept of strategic management: the design school – strategy as a process of conception; the planning school – strategy as a formal process; the positioning school – strategy as an analytical process; the entrepreneurial school – strategy as a visionary process; the cognitive school – strategy as a mental process; the learning school – strategy as an emergent process; the power school – strategy as a process of negotiation; the cultural school – strategy as a collective process; the environmental school – strategy as a reactive process; the configuration school – strategy as a process of transformation.[8] Therefore, it is logical to assume that given the abundance of choice in strategic thought, individuals within the firm may not agree on a single approach to strategy. One could argue that the first challenge that the strategist must come to grips with is a common understanding of the process of strategy formulation and a fundamental knowledge of the various schools of strategic thought. The second challenge is to assess which approach to strategy development best suits the firm under the present business conditions. Adopting a multidimensional view of strategy makes the strategic individual valuable as a lynchpin in the proliferation of the concept of a strategic mindset throughout the firm. In order for individuals to play this pivotal role in how the corporation engages in developing a strategic competency, it is vital to gain an understanding of the fundamentals of the strategic mindset, which is the subject of the next chapter.

Developing the strategic mindset

> *Axiom: The strategic mindset consists of thinking skills that enable the core competency of the firm, which is made relevant by a business context.*

People within the organization must adopt a mindset that puts the execution of strategy into everyday thinking throughout the firm. In order to meet the new competitive environment, the formulation of today's strategies, the execution of strategic initiatives and the tactical decisions that are a product of adjusting strategic intentions must become second nature to people within the organization. However, strategy development is a process that operates in parallel with the firm's business processes; it should not be perceived as a separate and discreet activity such as 'it's time for the strategy meetings'. Strategic thinking is not a typical skill found within the organization; it must be developed. Strategy must be a seamless process that acts solely to support the business process as it transitions from the present set of operating conditions to a future state of operations. Most people are engaged in day-to-day activities and are often faced with immediate problems such as survival, production delays, inventory shortages, cash flow interruptions, competitive shortfalls and other events that act to disrupt the normal course of business and consider strategy development as someone else's problem. Even fewer people believe that they can afford the luxury of taking time to look at daily activity in the context of a larger corporate agenda. Simply put, many organizations are so busy at finding the solutions that they cannot make time to investigate the cause in order to prevent future occurrences.

For Ray Grime, from the Bank of Bermuda, strategy development in corporations today must be the product of a process that aggregates creative out-of-the-box thinking across the firm and not simply a plan developed by an elite set of people at the top of a company:

> Strategy should be in the mindset of all employees and should be a part of the entire company process. Company processes should be built and implemented to make this a reality. Employees should regularly ask themselves several key questions:
>
> • Why do we do it this way?
> • How can we do it better?
> • How can we add value?
> • How can we provide better service to clients?
> • How can I get my clients more engaged in what we are doing or are going to do?

Grime elaborates that the company must act proactively in a strategic manner by formalizing and rewarding a way of thinking that results in establishing the strategy development process as an integral part of the company's culture, both internally and externally. Therefore, one can argue that strategic thinking rarely occurs naturally within the organization and in the past had to be imposed on the organization by people who were semi-detached from the day-to-day process of the business. In today's economic climate, however, strategy must be more dynamic than in previous generations of business and the process of strategy development must be more closely coupled with the everyday business process. Dynamic strategy development requires an individual to simultaneously think strategically as well as tactically. Often this dualistic approach to strategy development can be accomplished merely by placing tactical decisions into a strategic context. In many cases, management teams need to establish a process for strategy development in

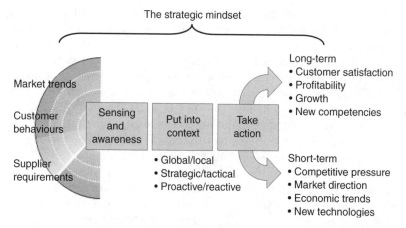

Figure 2.1   The strategic mindset

conjunction with a process to develop strategic thinking skills. At the nexus between a process for strategy development and the cultivation of strategic thinking skills is an individual's ability to embrace the strategic mindset, as depicted in Figure 2.1.

Adopting the mindset requires that the organization leverage each individual's ability to place day-to-day issues into a framework that includes sensing market trends, customer behaviours and supplier requirements while placing them into a context which is derived from corporate goals and objectives. Once in context, each business issue must be categorized into either a long-term or short-term action item. Subsequently, a solution must be developed within the resources of the firm. In this process, the role of the management team is that of resource prioritization.

Sensing and awareness

As individuals within the firm are increasingly overloaded with more and more data and information originating from sources inside and outside the company, the process of sorting information to find its specific relevance becomes more time consuming. It is critical to be able to sense changes in the marketplace, such as new pricing by competitors, sudden changes in international regulation and other market activity which in many cases is beyond the control of the corporation. Data to characterize which changes must then be compared to existing strategic initiatives to either validate the firm's course or used to take corrective actions. To keep abreast of customer behaviour, companies in most cases have to develop either a feedback process or rely on external sources or both.

As products change, alliances are formed, and capabilities are outsourced. The requirements of suppliers are a factor that must be integrated into the strategic planning process because in the case of outsourcing it becomes one of the constraining resources. Developing market awareness and creating a process that acts like corporate radar to sense and detect changes in the business environment is essential as we will see in detail in the section 'Sensing the market, competitors, customers and opportunities'.

Putting information, data and events into context

Once an organization has established a process that senses the marketplace, customers and suppliers, the information from that process must be placed in the context of the corporate goals and objectives. A strategic context requires a vision, which in turn establishes a direction for the firm to apply its resources, as noted by Ralph:

> Vision for an organization is one level above goals or objectives; it is more general and more deeply felt. Leadership is necessary to get others to fulfil that vision. Leadership is displayed in establishing the conditions and incentives necessary to realise the vision. It taps into the need latent in every human being; the need to feel they are valued; that they can make a difference. Then they will.[9]

Corporate visions must be clearly understood by everyone in the organization and communicated to employees, customers and suppliers. Richard Tannahill, from GlaxoSmithKline, makes an important point that in order to think strategically and take action, a firm must first know where the organization is going.

> For a strategy to be effective, it must be credible, understood by the entire organization, and actionable. To be implemented by the organization either as a whole, or in part, strategy requires a roadmap and the implementers must also have the strategic mindset.

Tannahill explains that every organization is on a journey in which strategy is the articulation of the place on the map where one wants to get to; strategy should not be confused with the route or action plan that we wish to take to get there. Strategy has a greater chance of successful implementation when it is developed by a wider group of people within the firm and not restricted to the senior leadership team alone. In Tannahill's view, strategy is futuristic in its outlook, but it is also grounded in an assessment of the past. Strategy is built on the knowledge of the organization in which a vision of the future is created based on an analysis of the external and internal environment. An organization requires specific skills to be able to develop a strategy; it requires a strategic mindset.

Tannahill reminds us of a key implication of the strategic mindset that once a strategy has been developed it must cascade down the organization in a way that triggers operating groups within the firm to develop their own action plans. When relating how and what should be communicated to the organization, Tannahill provides us with an example from General George S. Patton: 'Never tell people how to do things. Tell them what to do and they will surprise you with their ingenuity.'[10] The implication of this line of thinking is that once the strategic mindset has been achieved, management can trust the organization to develop rational ideas and reasonable actions. Tannahill describes an organization as having a soul or culture and a learned way of thinking, surviving when it has a clear sense of direction or strategy. When an organization realizes this, it has a strategic mindset.

Taking action with strategic initiatives and tactical manoeuvres

The process of strategy development is complete when it generates successive sets of strategic initiatives which in and of themselves initiate tactical manoeuvres that make the strategy actionable by default. Taking action is purely a result of strategy execution, and unfortunately has the potential to generate new problems which might be contrary to the designed strategic intent. For example, the methodology for business process re-engineering projects typically results in initiatives that fall into three distinct categories: long-term or strategic efforts, short-term or tactical activities and low-hanging fruit or actions that can be taken immediately to achieve a quick result. Organizations driven to produce quarterly results and news regardless of the long-term implications found that re-engineering projects that identified low-hanging fruit in many cases produced instant results, which were more palatable, and that long-term strategic initiatives required greater justification and scrutiny. In extreme cases, this low-hanging fruit evolved into 'management cocaine', that is, the projects were encouraged to forego the strategic initiatives whilst they continuously produced quick fixes.

Developing and nurturing the strategic mindset

The prerequisite for engaging a strategic mindset is to create a process in which people within the firm acquire and update strategic thinking skills at regular intervals. Figure 2.2 illustrates the process that

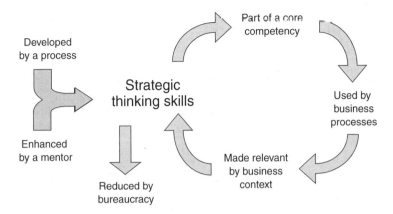

Figure 2.2   Strategic thinking skills

must exist within the firm to continually nurture skills in order to make strategy second nature to people in front-line management. Skill development is an iterative process and not a training event. Skills must be developed in such a way that people can immediately practise their new knowledge in ways that allow them to see how their knowledge is made relevant to day-to-day business problems. This line of thinking is akin to Albert Einstein's famous quotation, 'The significant problems we face cannot be solved at the same level of thinking we were at when we created them.'[11]

Changing a corporate culture and altering the collective mindset of the firm is by no means an easy undertaking. It also requires a strategy due to its complex nature as Eric Grunwald, from Perihelion, explains:

> Here is a warning about the difficulty of changing mindsets: In 1966, Yoko Ono designed a chess set. It was an unconventional chess set – all the pieces were white and the intention was to change the metaphor of chess from war and conflict to unity and harmony. You were supposed to go on playing until you could not remember whose pieces were whose. Unfortunately, painting black pieces white does not change mindsets; just creates confusion.

One could argue that altering a firm's mindset requires each person within the firm to develop to some degree a fundamental understanding of strategic thinking skills. Kevan Jones, of Corven, has a view that a mindset is what must be developed over time; it is not done quickly like a frontal lobotomy or a religious conversion. In Jones' view, changing the mindset of an organization takes time, commitment and determination. Alternatively, a company can rapidly instigate a change in mindset by either buying another firm or poach a significant number of talented people from a competitor. Using this approach the change in personnel acts as a catalyst which can be used to initiate a change. In all cases, possessing a fundamental understanding of strategic thinking skills is a prerequisite to changing the corporate mindset as illustrated in Figure 2.2.

Applying strategic thinking skills to a process that continually aligns strategy with changing business objectives demands that skills be formed into centres of competencies. Competence formation is vital to leverage skills during times in which a change in business conditions requires radically new approaches to traditional problems such as when a new market entrant brings to the market a product that revolutionizes the industry. Grime notes that understanding the firm's current competencies and contrasting them against the competencies required to execute the components of a strategy is often a set missed by companies during the strategy development process. According to Grime the opportunity exists for organizations to tap into the company's greatest asset, their employees, engaging their minds and bodies to guarantee staff commitment. The strategic mindset is threefold: to hold the belief that what is being done is correct, to have customers passionate about the company and to engage the staff emotionally.

Grime points out that strategies and individual strategic thinking skills are not simply linked to capabilities and that skills are inexorably combined to form a corporate competency. The implication that employees are used as the cornerstone for strategy development, is also remarked upon by Lloyd, who states that strategy is a process of adapting to changes in the business environment.

> Strategy is of course about change, purposeful change and purposeful response to change. Strategy development involves every type of physical and organizational asset as well as human and intellectual resources. Strategy development implies change, which fosters a fresh understanding, and/or altered motivation, leading to changed capability and/or changed behaviour.

This is a key point, because many organizations fail when they create strategies that do not anticipate alterations to business conditions that may leave their strategy invalid. Like the strategies themselves, strategic thinking skills are also in a state of continuous change and although the fundamentals of strategy development remain similar, the techniques and methods used to keep the strategy current must change to keep pace with the evolution of business. The most effective method for developing strategic thinking skills is that of mentoring, as noted by Lloyd.

Without change, development is absent. However, change implies risk, uncertainty, cost and threat, and tends to be avoided or minimised. So how do we develop the strategic mindset in the firm? We do so by the variety of learning mechanisms such as formal briefings and training courses, learning by doing, on-the-job experience, all hopefully enhanced by feedback from the supervisor and colleagues, perhaps with mentor support. Personal reflection is also vital: on one's own experience, on the experience of others, perhaps prompted by feedback, preparation for an appraisal or by acting as a mentor, or as a result of something read or viewed.

The aforementioned types of learning are leveraged in three ways: by spotting patterns, subconsciously by following a role model (probably the most powerful and most overlooked learning mechanism in any group) or by developing and following new procedures.

Building on Lloyd's point, Shaharazad Abuel-Ealeh, from Career Research and Advisory Council (CRAC), explains that strategic thinking as a key skill rather than a mindset or a culture allows simpler management of employee expectations. Adopting a strategic mindset implies that employees are expected to balance strategic and tactical objectives. The important outcome of this is that employee driven strategies allow for flexibility, enabling a strategy to change, while realizing the expectation that the workforce will adapt to the new strategic intentions.

Mentors and leaders

Individuals have an inherent need for a role model as Dodson notes: 'Leadership is an elusive concept, hard to describe and impossible to prescribe. It is more evident in its absence, so that when leadership is needed, its lack is sorely felt.'[12] When discussing leadership in the context of how organizations must adapt to new business conditions, Stuart Bradley of Corven recalls the conversations that supported a comparison between Darwinism and the influences of the business environment on organizations. The principles that Darwin articulated, regarding how a species can adapt to new environments or change to take increasing advantage of existing environments – frequently, and erroneously, called 'the survival of the fittest' – appear to match well some observations of the business world. However, if we extrapolate this analogy, there are some interesting implications.

In Bradley's view, the nature of Darwinian change is that of mutation of the genetic code of individuals. Over vast periods, if these mutations prove to confer some advantage to individuals that translates into an enhanced position in the species community, they gradually make changes to the entire species and with the subsequent improvement of the outcome in the reproductive process. For example, during the industrial revolution in Britain, it was proven that certain species of butterflies changed at the genetic level such that they became more efficiently disguised in the natural environment, and therefore less obvious to predators. Random black markings on white wings replicating the sooty deposits that abounded in industrialized Britain, allowed the butterflies with these markings to blend better into their environment. Over generations, such markings became prevalent, and the species changed because of individual butterflies surviving and passing on their specific genetic codes. However, unlike business, the process of Darwinian evolution did not occur based on a deliberate process with measured outcomes. This must also be taken into consideration because although we recognize that gradual change lessens the trauma on an organization, we also must acknowledge that within the evolution analogy, species such as penguins did not hold meetings to debate evolution or discuss the most effective routes of migration.[13] Penguins did not deliberately architect change; evolution happened unknown to them.

Here again, Bradley reminds us to remember that the mutation of butterfly DNA was entirely random. It had nothing to do with external influences, and came about quite by chance. This is the nature of Darwinism: mutations are chance events, but nature decides which individuals survive and which do not. Therefore, the influence of the environment is not on the mutation, but rather on the survival of the individual. Of course, sometimes we do see the environment creating mutations – nuclear radiation is an example, but in most cases mutation is a chance internal phenomenon.

According to Bradley, there are several key implications for strategy development. If the analogy is completely appropriate, then attempts at strategy development really are futile; an arrogant attempt to 'play God'. We might conclude that the changes to organizations should come about from entirely random mutations – it is how the organism responds to the changing environment that determines success. The role of leadership would therefore be to maximize the chance of hitting the right mutation by encouraging change at all levels of the organization on a continual basis. Of course, the down side to this is that mutations are frequently conferring disadvantage onto the organism, which would suggest within the context of business that a leader's role should be to avoid change completely. Perhaps the Darwinist analogy is imperfect – perhaps there are things that leaders can do to speed up the selection of mutations that are likely to confer advantage, a sort of husbandry approach. The leader's role is therefore not necessarily to stimulate organizational mutation, but to intervene in a way that he/she believes will speed up the growth and assimilation of organizational change that confers qualities that make it better suited to the environment. Either way, it is all about mutation, so any leader unable to handle that, is unlikely to be able to improve the organization's chance of getting its genes back into the gene pool.

Bradley makes a key distinction in that today's leaders must guide or direct an organization by establishing operational boundaries; they do not act as a control point. This view is shared by Loton: 'Tomorrow's leaders must be prepared to facilitate achievement by others. This means giving people more control over their own work. Less direct management of those working for you, and more emphasis on their training and building their confidence are required.'[14]

To most organizations, the Chief Executive Officer (CEO) and the senior management team are a source of inspiration and usually set the tone for the behaviour of the firm. In the business climate that is carrying over from the last quarter of the twentieth century, a CEO's length of tenure can be a significant factor in the execution of strategy and, more important, understanding the results. David Doyle, of Prudential plc, puts it this way:

Analytical research shows that shareholder value is most often created where the CEO and senior management team have served a significant period of tenure within the company. Frequently, they will have been elevated to the CEO role after having fulfilled a number of other roles in the company. That CEOs of some length of tenure add the most value is not surprising when one considers that the process of change (together with the incumbent cultural change) is also a medium- to long-term process.

In Doyle's view, this fact is alarming news in the current environment of ever-shortening CEO tenures, frequently driven by exposures of corporate 'fat cattery' in the press. Institutional shareholders who themselves are also increasingly subject to ever-shorter-term performance monitoring are failing companies and ultimately themselves and all other stakeholders by driving CEOs to short-term tactical moves to hit earnings targets at the cost of material damage to the company's long-term growth prospects. Doyle postulates that it is possible that a seemingly relentless pressure will drive talented executives towards pursuing careers in private companies away from the scrutiny of institutional shareholders, activist groups, the public and press.

The implications of a constantly swinging CEO door, in Doyle's perspective, is that they end up with little time to introduce effective long-lasting change, and eventually fall into the downward spiral of rounds of cost-cutting which, while probably successful in the short term, slowly strangles the company's investment and growth opportunities. Ultimately, the organization is taken over or fails from neglect. Therefore, investors and the press need to develop a more modern dialogue with companies looking for CEO skills beyond pure ego and charisma and understand what really drives the CEO and how they look at an organization. Equally, companies and CEOs need to engage more honestly with investors on the strategic challenges that they face.

Leadership does not have to be tied to a single personality

An alternative view to the CEO as a focal point for the organization is articulated by Abuel-Ealeh in the example of the Future Directions – University of Warwick Students' Union, which has a staff of 100 full-time and 300 part-time employees and an annual turnover in excess of £5 million pounds.[15] The Student Union operates seven bars, five restaurants, three nightclubs and three retail outlets, which makes it a small- to medium-size business in its own right. What is interesting to note is that the leadership of the organization changes every year because officers elected act as trustees and company directors. Future Directions was the result of a 14-month consultation period with all major stakeholders: permanent staff, part-time student officers, full-time student officers, customers and the university. This case study illustrates what happens when you instil the strategic mindset too rigidly, and how eventually it has a negative effect on staff–volunteer morale; it is expanded below.

In Abuel-Ealeh's view, one of the most positive aspects of this environment is the willingness of staff and officers to take on major challenges, and in such a relatively large Student Union, it was vital that a coherent strategy was developed. Why? Obviously because the Student Union functions as a business, but more importantly due to its reliance on students who want to get actively involved, and take on responsibility for running the organization.

As Abuel-Ealeh points out, the key problem encountered by Future Directions was with the leadership of the organization. While the strategy may well have been input by the majority of the organization, and significant efforts had been made to equip the individuals with the knowledge and skills needed to input into the process, the leaders of the organization (full-time elected officers) did not necessarily understand the value of the contributions received or of the exercise itself – as they had not themselves been part of the original team championing the exercise.

Alongside this, many stakeholders were insincere in their support for 'Future Directions' – simply as a result of the vague notion that, since it was important, people should know about it. However, not enough people understood what it was that was being promoted, or why. For those that did understand, there was a lack of genuine leadership or 'championing of the cause'. Abuel-Ealeh notes that by the time all of the leadership were on board – which eventually happened – the staff and volunteers had lost faith in the process and the documentation for the exercise had simply become mere archive material.

Other than the vast waste of time, money and resources that went into the process (and for the bulk it was a waste – how useful is a strategy that is three–four years old and has never been acted on?), the significant effect of this process was the difficulty that would be encountered by future generations who would want to implement a collaborative strategic approach. While the leadership may change year on year, the staff and to some extent the volunteers do not. Of course, this is quite a specific example. Organizational leadership is usually more stable outside of the university student context; however, the basic premise remains: equipping the workforce with the skill of strategic planning (i.e. the strategic mindset) makes it more important than ever that strong leadership and vision should exist in order to ensure that employees do not become disillusioned with the strategic process.

Both Doyle and Abuel-Ealeh identify that company morale is a factor easily underestimated in the traditional strategic planning process and must be cultivated by the senior management team. As more decision-making capabilities are disbursed into line organizations, morale becomes a mechanism for senior managers to increase productivity. Linked closely to morale are motivation and mentoring, which together act as principle means for senior managers to engage the strategic planning process. A process for strategy development and effective

Unmotivated individual	Motivated individual	Strategic individual
• No achievable goals • No recognition of success • Unclear definition of role with the wider context of the company • No understanding of corporate goals	• Clearly defined short-term financial targets • Recognition of success • Clearly defined role • Limited need to understand company goals and implications within the company	• Clearly defined short-term financial targets • Recognition of success • Clearly defined role • Understanding of company goals and importance of role • Ability to effect working environment
• No achievable targets	• Short-term financial/other goals	• Balanced targets • Short term to long term • Financial to strategic

Figure 2.3   Strategy and the individual

mentoring by leaders is a tremendous advantage over most firms, but many organizations require two additional elements: motivation and investment.

Motivation

Motivation does not always translate to direct compensation. Sarah Byrne-Quinn from Cable & Wireless plc describes motivation in the context of strategy development as a means to influence people such that they then become self-motivated. Achieving a strategic mindset is what motivates an individual to perform his/her job, but taking it further, a strategic individual does not work for a company, he/she participates in the success of a company as outlined in Figure 2.3.

Byrne-Quinn provides us with an example of the results that are possible when individuals are motivated to participate in the successes of a company – the 'strategic' individual can be seen in every industry regardless of geography.

Example: call centre employee

Unmotivated
- He clocks in at exactly 9:00.
- He uses the tools he has been trained to use.
- He has unrealistic goals of 60 calls per hour that he knows he will miss so he goes for 30 calls an hour which he knows is the minimum to keep his job.

- His lack of understanding of the company leaves him with no empathy for the customer he talks to, he is abrupt and only answers the questions asked.
- He leaves at 5:00 and views work as a necessary evil in his life.

Motivated

- He clocks in at 9:00.
- He is well trained on the tools he has been provided and understands how to use the tools to meet his daily targets.
- His targets are at a stretch 50 calls an hour, but he meets these targets 60 per cent of the time and the bonuses he gets are timely and worth the effort.
- He understands that he has some control over his work performance and the impact this has on his financial well-being.
- The company has very cost effective and efficient call centres bid customers as their calls get answered quickly and their questions are addressed.

Strategic

- He clocks in at 9:00.
- He has a good understanding of the goals of the company and the importance of his job to those goals.
- He uses the tools he is provided with and his knowledge of the company's goals and his job to help the company meet customer needs and help customers solve their problems – it is not about just answering questions.
- His goals include a balance of achievable targets including number of calls per minute.
- The company's strategic goals need to align with the individual's for this to happen:
  - Aligned strategic and financial goals.
  - Ability to effect change.
  - Trust and more communication.

In Byrne-Quinn's example, we see that motivation is not created simply by the establishment of rules in which a person must operate; it is the result of an ongoing dialogue between the company and the individual based on communication and feedback that supports an individual's role within a strategic context as depicted in Figure 2.4.

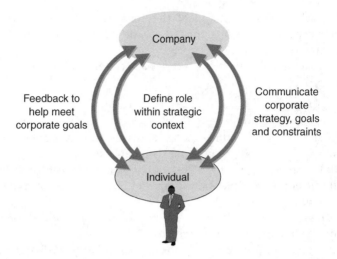

Figure 2.4   Strategy, the company and the individual

Investment

Individuals must develop skills that enable them to actively assess and improve the company's value proposition. According to Abuel-Ealeh, the skills act in concert with components that make up the company's core competency to achieve the expressed goals of a firm. Therefore, it surely follows that a workforce that understands the value of strategy also has the ability to work in ways that complement a strategic plan. Employees who have adopted a strategic mindset and have the confidence to offer strategic thinking at every level of the organization will be more productive workforce.

In Abuel-Ealeh's view, to get the workforce up to this level of strategic competency, a major investment must be made – in time, money and human resources. If it is given that there is a strategic aim to invest these resources in the organization's people, the efforts to do so should stimulate and motivate the participants, as well as efficiently articulate exactly why the organization considers this key. Importantly, it must place this activity within the organization's strategic context – how does this activity fit in with the bigger picture?

Abuel-Ealeh believes that corporations should ask themselves key questions:

- Is your workforce ready for this kind of shift in perceptions?
- What are the learning styles of your workforce? What is the preferred means of communicating this kind of message?

- Is the leadership ready to open the floodgate?
- Does your organization have the means to incorporate the subsequent input from its employees?
- Can you perceive the benefits of a workforce with a strategic mindset?
- Do you REALLY want your entire workforce to have the strategic mindset?

Abuel-Ealeh makes a good point that investments in people are not just a prerequisite for initiating the development of a strategic mindset, periodic investments are imperative to continue the momentum generated by the organization that is engaged in developing dynamic strategies. Continual investment and constant motivation are essential ingredients in the strategic thinking process that raises the question of who pays for continuous education, the corporation or the individual. If learning is fundamental to developing strategic thinking skills, should corporations consider training and education expense items or investments?

Bureaucracy

Figure 2.5 reminds us that bureaucracy is a relentless force that acts to retard an organization's ability to achieve a strategic mindset. Nick Coyle

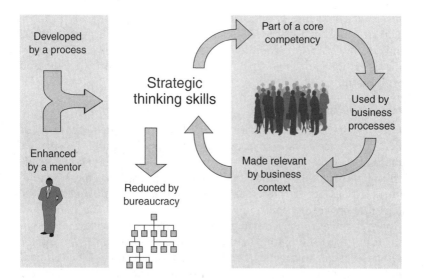

Figure 2.5 Bureaucracy and the strategic mindset

of Corven presents us with a view that in the future, every individual should play a role in developing and adapting the strategy of the organization to which they belong. Indeed, in Coyle's view, there is a growing trend for stakeholders at all levels to participate in developing and adapting the strategy of the organization, be it a Small to Medium-Sized Enterprise (SME), a large Multinational, or a not-for-profit organization. This recognizes the importance and multiple statuses of individuals who can be employees, customers, investors and others, simultaneously.

The globalization of competition, according to Coyle, means that organizations must coordinate actions across continents and large differences in time. It also means that they must react with speed and tailor their products and services to local markets. No competitive position is sustainable indefinitely, and changes must be made. This requires that organizations should develop new strategies to deal with this. These new strategies also require changes in the way in which organizations organize themselves to do their work. Bureaucratic command-and-control structures are not designed to enable the strategies that the future necessitates, the strategies that empower individuals to make changes, and the strategies which enable individuals to contribute to the direction of the organization. Bureaucratic command-and-control structures lend themselves to compartmentalization, to narrow functional thinking that leads to suboptimal decisions being taken. The challenge is to develop and embrace new types of organization structures that place greater emphasis on speed of decision making, and create a sense of ownership for the individuals involved. Ownership may be real or imagined, arising out of a sense of identity, loyalty and enthusiasm.

Mindset versus bureaucracy

John Dembitz, from Boyden Global Executive Search, reminds us that bureaucracies can act in two distinct ways restricting the strategic mindset and alternatively enhancing its adoption by leveraging people within the firm. It is true that in most organizations, the structural bureaucracies act to erect barriers to free/creative thinking and the organization creates constraints to the questioning of the status quo. However, once convinced that any new strategy is in the best interest of the firm's goals and objectives, the bureaucracy within the organizations can be leveraged to encourage and reward new and desirable behavioural traits such as openness, active participation, constructive criticism and asking questions such as why are we doing things a certain way.

In Dembitz's view, there is no such thing as hierarchy for the development of ideas; leaders such as Michael Dell, Bill Gates, Richard Branson and Steve Jobs were all in their late teens or early twenties when they got started and were not encumbered by rigid organizations. Traditional organization structures constrain/limit/block the early development of strategic mindset presenting a challenge for senior managers who must act to guide strategic thinking through the organization. Here again, Dembitz makes a strong point that traditional Human Relations departments are agents of limitation rather than facilitators of change or adoption of new ideas. The key point that Dembitz makes is that in order for the strategic mindset to be developed in a bureaucracy it requires a catalyst, which in many cases must originate from the senior management team.

Collaboration

One final aspect of the strategic mindset is probably the single most difficult skill to master in the business environment offered by the twenty-first century, that of effective collaboration. Collaboration presents today's business and indeed the strategic individual with the dilemma of how and what is collaboration and what is competition. In the view of Peter Parker, of EPCot Systems, to develop a mindset for strategy it is essential not to work alone. There are so many concepts to keep in mind that the strategic mind must be open to many concepts simultaneously to derive a dynamic strategy. Whilst the strategic mind may be (but is not necessarily) in one person, the process is best served by involving others within the organization. This collaboration will deliver more robust and more encompassing strategies than an isolationist approach.

Parker relates an example used when developing a strategy for a UK government agency. At that time, it was essential to involve regulation, registry, finance, policy and marketing in constructing the strategy. Missing out on any one of these would have left a serious gap in the final delivery process and in the underlying strategy. In working this strategy, the different mindsets and points of view involved amply illustrated the value gained by using a collaborative approach. In Parker's view, a strategic mindset is that of a visionary creating and laying out the overall setting for future plans. One of the participants was a person who paid particular attention to detail and her contribution ensured that the strategy did not lose some of the areas that were essential to a successful strategy. Similarly, another colleague was useful in knitting strands of the business together. Her contribution would be to show the commonality of various apparently dissimilar threads. It would be simple to say that the mindset for strategy could all be found in one head, or else that it is a matter of learning the toolset. However, like a meeting, delivering a strategy requires a chairperson, who clarifies objectives and sets the agenda, an ideas person who is a source of original ideas and a finisher who checks details and meets deadlines.[16]

To elaborate on Parker's view, Coyle pointed out that the means by which individuals can collaborate and contribute to strategic decisions, processes, must be developed, employing technology where appropriate, but also providing face-to-face personal interaction and debate. This can only begin to take place once training has been undertaken. This training must act as a baptism for the organization, bringing everyone up to the basic level of understanding to enable an individual to make informed decisions with regard to the alternatives and to the consequences. However, as Coyle noted, there will probably be a hierarchy of training requirements. There will still be individuals who will carry more responsibility and be in positions where they need to have a better understanding of strategy, how it is arrived at and how to influence it. These individuals need better, more in-depth training. The training should also be of a continuous nature in order to ensure that everyone is capable of contributing.

Coyle also presents us with an alternative view of how every individual behaves strategically. Strategy is a matter of resolution; fundamentally, every issue, whether it relates to the organization as a whole, or to the task of an individual in a department or function, will be answered in terms of 'what' and 'how'. What are we going to do (about this), and how are we going to do it (from amongst the different alternatives)? Here, 'what' represents the strategy, and 'how' is the means by which the issue will be solved. To the organization, answering the question 'what products shall we produce in future, and what markets shall we compete in?' will go some way to providing a strategy. This will be followed by how shall we produce them and how will we compete? However, at a lower level of resolution, to those charged with producing and marketing, the answer to how they will be produced and how they will compete becomes a 'what', to be answered by another more detailed 'how'. Therefore, for the individual faced with dealing with a problematic customer, what he decides to do, and how he decides to do it, represents a strategy and operational tactics that may, depending upon the importance of the customer, or the number of times he/she has to deal with this problem, represent strategic decisions to the organizations as a whole.

The key point that Parker and Coyle bring out is that individuals must use their strategic mindset to interpret changing business conditions both to respond to customers' demands and to act as stimulus in recalibrating the firm's strategy. Not all business change will initiate a corresponding change in strategy. Therefore, individuals must filter and interpret each change as to its relevance to the overall strategy.

Engaging the strategic mindset

Is it perhaps the case that organizations do not need to develop a 'stategic mindset' formally, argues Abuel-Ealeh. The organization may simply require another essential skill, such as problem solving, communication and the ability to work in teams. A prudent move for a company is to proactively poll and determine which skills employees need to develop.

Abuel-Ealeh continues to explain that a major implication of equipping people with strategic thinking skills and ultimately with a strategic mindset is that unless the leadership of the organization provides a mechanism through which employees can genuinely input into the organization's strategic plan, the effort is wasted. This mechanism must also exist within each strategic initiative and for the tactical aspects of the plan. In this case, one must consider how the expectations of the workforce are to be managed; for the process of strategy development to benefit from employees using their strategic thinking skills it must be promoted as a tangible way through which employees can influence the direction of the organization. If this is the case, employees are equipped to offer a means through which change can be implemented. Is there a better – or more realistic – way to present the strategic mindset to your workforce?

As Abuel-Ealeh rightly contends, once strategic thinking skills are in place, they must be used in conjunction with the pre-existing business process. In many cases, the establishment of the strategic mindset also triggers other implications for organizations to consider:

- Is the leadership prepared to share its strategic responsibility?
- Is there an effective means of doing this?
- Could your employees be less satisfied with their workplace because of being more skilled?
- Could your employees expect more rapid promotion?
- Will there be sufficient means through which your employees can take on more responsibility for their own roles, teams and departments?

Behaviour is linked to mindset

The key to moving the strategic mindset into practice within the firm, according to Coyle, is to link it directly to behaviour. When linked, strategy then becomes an aggregation of the actions and decisions taken by individuals at all levels across the organization, ever changing and fluid, responsive to the environment. To do this of course requires more than just a change of structure; it requires a change in the mindset of top management and every individual within the organization, a recasting of each person's role. Only by changing mindsets will behaviours change. In order to enable this, systemic changes need to be made to the organization. The change in structure and the alteration in expectation around roles require changes to skills, so as to equip individuals with the ability to put into action the role they must perform. This must be supported by changes to the ways in which management actually manages individuals, the structures and methods employed. In turn, this must be reinforced by the appropriate measurement and reward systems to provide a 'carrot and stick' for new behaviours.

Coyle explains that as the organization adapts to deliver the new strategies, the changes described above are made, so the norms, values and beliefs of the organization will slowly change to reflect the new context. This facet must be designed in the same way as the other assets of the organization. It is in this area that senior management plays an important lead, providing role models for the new behaviours, not least in the development of trust. Last, but by no means least, changes to processes, technology and the provision of information complete the series of changes that are necessary to deliver the organization where individuals can act strategically.

Conclusion

The problem of adopting a strategic mindset is summed up well by David Shirreff, from *The Economist*. If the individual itself were a corporation, there would be no problem about developing a strategic mindset. Even changing nothing would amount to a strategy for the one-person corporation. Nevertheless, when two or more people form an organization, there begins to be a need to align strategy and to communicate it throughout the organization. Otherwise, a gap opens up between the leadership, which by default makes strategy, and free riders, who do their job but are not contributing feedback to the strategy pursued by the company. Leaders can make things worse by ignoring what those at the coalface of those with direct contact to customers, suppliers and so on, could tell them.

Here Shirreff makes a key point as companies or organizations grow, communication must continue. The process is not automatic. It must be fostered by encouraging individuals to engage in the development of strategy, if they are so inclined, or at least by keeping the individuals, who are not so inclined, informed about strategy. A nice example is of two stone masons working side by side who are asked about their work; one says he is carving a stone, the other says he is making a cathedral. Even in the extreme case of a belligerent organization, such as company soldiers, it is questionable whether the soldier blindly doing what he is told is a better military instrument than the one who is aware of the higher objective. In Shirreff's view, people who see the big picture are probably more trustworthy and valuable. The nuclear disaster at Chernobyl might have been worse, had not a handful of brave workers sacrificed their lives to mitigate the meltdown.

Therefore, strategic thinking in an organization must be a two-way process. It should not be the result of management reaching down, but just as much of an engaged workforce, and middle management, looking up, down and around in all directions. This can only be achieved if the process of dynamic strategy formulation is one of the declared objectives of the company and a conscious part of firms' procedures.

Embracing a global context

Axiom: Senior managements are the mentors to people and provide an understanding of the broader global context of strategic issues.

It has been argued elsewhere that the continual evolution of telecommunications technologies has ushered in a new era in which all businesses, large and small, are now engaged in some form of global commerce, either by desire or as a result of being an unwilling competitor in a worldwide marketplace.[17] Businesses are beginning to realize that the new nature of competition centres on delivering on a value proposition and not a specific product or service. Products and services are susceptible to the changes in consumer demand and therefore should be considered temporary. The endurance of a product is directly proportional to its perception of value in the marketplace multiplied by the market or consumer awareness of the product. Therefore, the long-term viability of a corporation is its ability to deliver changing products and services within a price that is perceived to be valuable by customers. The consistent delivery of products and services within an operating framework that optimizes cost and fulfils customer's needs is a core competency that must be developed and is the fundamental building block for strategy development. All firms regardless of size and location have the opportunity to engage in commerce on a global scale. Domestic frictions can develop between local people and the corporation when the idiosyncrasies of the culture are ignored out of hand as unimportant which is also true globally as noted by Giddens: 'Many business leaders do not act as full citizens, since they ignore the social outcomes of their business decisions.'[18] Corporations operating internationally under a multinational organizational structure permit individual subsidiaries to act autonomously within their domestic markets using a multi-domestic strategy in which some functions are centralized with the headquarters such as research and development, information systems, marketing, purchasing and finance while other functions such as sales are carried out entirely at the domestic level.[19] In order to address the challenges that global competition brings, corporations and, more importantly, individuals within the corporate lines of business must develop broadly an understanding of the factors that influence commerce, customers and their behaviour. Day describes the global market realities as having six fundamental characteristics: customer-accepting standardized products that offer superior value of local customized products, diversification of supply chains from global sourcing, competitors cross-subsidizing to gain entry into a market, liberalization of trade and the advance of technology.[20] These characteristics are influenced by the cultural diversities found in the geographies in which they operate. Grime points out that corporations cannot ignore the global context in which they operate and, as such, the global context should be built into the strategic thinking. According to Grime, when developing competitive strategies, it is essential that companies should recognize the differences in cultures and ways of doing business in different countries: 'What one company can do in one given country and the effects of its action to the business are not necessarily the same if the same strategy is applied to another country.'

Grime relates an example of this culture-focused mentality in the Hong Kong and Shanghai Banking Corporation (HSBC), which has introduced the first high-street mortgage plan for Muslims taking into account the fact that according to Islamic law, Muslims are not allowed to pay or receive interest. In Grime's view, global companies need to ensure that their organizations are networked and that they have good market intelligence and business information about the country markets where they wish to enter so that the strategic plan can be put in place. Another good example is Sony's alliance strategy when the company started developing an overseas operation. Sony ensured that the local alliances would sell and distribute their products and once the products were established, they would set up their own shops and distribution networks.

Dembitz elaborates on the need to incorporate cultural aspects into strategic planning by discussing the approach of Shell Oil, one of the world's leading multinational corporations. Shell's CEO, N. Fitzgerald, is focused on moving the company into becoming truly global by what he has termed making it become 'multi local'. Dembitz argues that if a corporation really thinks this through, the implications to the markets they serve, the operations of the business and the coordination of resources are enormous. Companies such as Shell used to send their British/Dutch executives to run their business around the world, all of the top positions were filled by executives that came through the ranks from the home base(s). But a gradual shift has taken place over the past decade or so, with an increasing number of Shell's senior executive positions being filled by non-Europeans, and the logical extension being to fully enfranchise all of Shell's employees, thereby becoming a truly global company, or a 'multi local'.

To place the strategic planning of the firm into a global context, it is important to establish first a framework in which a generic global strategy is developed, and from this baseline the strategy is modified to incorporate local idiosyncrasies. When firms attempt this approach they often make a misstep in that during the process of tailoring the many characteristics of the specific cultural marketplace, which should be considered tactical attributes suddenly become part of the strategic initiative. This phenomenon can be attributed to the fact that as the responsibility for strategic planning is delegated to lower and lower levels in the organization, individuals consciously or subconsciously use the strategy planning process to address immediate problems that tend to be tactical in nature. Grunwald explains that the difference between tactical and strategic thinking is the difference between blinkered and stereographic vision. The tactician will respond to events as they enter his restricted field of vision, and he will act solely in accordance with his own limited remit. He will 'get the job done' and be satisfied at the end of the day. To the strategic thinker, however, there are no boundaries either in space or in time. The strategist will always expand the boundaries of the field of his or her own responsibility to include events, changes, disruptions and trends from outside as well as the longer-term impacts of whatever he or she is considering doing.

The global context is just one of the broader viewpoints that must be reflected in today's strategies. Grunwald relates a personal experience from one of his previous employers which decided that it needed to 'go global'. The reasons for this were not entirely clear at the time the decision was made. On joining the company, when he asked why this was the company's strategy, he was told by a senior director that it was the only way of persuading good people to work for them. As a result of this distinctly non-global global strategy, the potential market for the company's products was analysed independently in many countries around the world. The best three potential markets were chosen for investment. One was in Europe, one was in the Middle East and the third was in the Far East. Therefore, the company's resources were stretched thinly around the world between three new businesses, each of which was individually too small to be of major importance.

Grunwald's example shows an essentially tactical attempt by a firm to become a global player. In each part of the globe, the new viewpoint was as limited as it had been in the home market. A more strategic version of the global context would have seen the broader analysis of regions of the world, probably resulting in the selection of one part of the globe that could have been entered in a coordinated, efficient way. A few isolated, apparently exciting small opportunities would – and should – have been spurned.

Four key factors

In a global context, the development of strategy is influenced by four key factors: external forces (such as new competitive pressures), globalization, disintermediation and the evolution of technology. As these external forces are internalized by the firm, they act to reshape continually how the organization behaves and approaches business activities such as servicing the customers, introducing new products and formulating relationships. Overall, the impact of these external forces changes the organization in three distinct areas: the structure of the organization, the focus of the firm's resources and the applied use of the firm's inherent skills in each person.

First, external factors are fostering a fundamental restructuring of the organization, not merely a realignment of the command-and-control hierarchy but a reorganization of the overall foundation in which the firm operates. During the 1990s, the traditional hierarchical organization began to migrate towards a more matrix line structure in which skills and capabilities aligned themselves functionally and independently of the lines of business. This realignment resulted in the formation of groups with similar skills concentrating the resources of the firm into highly specialized areas of capabilities. The establishment of capabilities that are independent of the line organization provides the firm with new levels of agility as they can readily reform the resources of the firm to take advantage of the new opportunities or solve problems with the existing line organization. The next evolution in a firm, which has a direct influence on the formulation of strategy, is a reformation of the organization as a network of interdependent cells of competencies. Competency in this sense is the combination of skills, capabilities and experience that form a cohesive ability.

Tannahill claims that as the competitive environment moves in favour of large organizations with transnational sales reach and consolidated purchasing power, the development of a strategy must always reflect a global view or at least view the company as a node in a global network of value added players. Tannahill observes that large organizations are increasingly moving away from a fully integrated local-country operation to an operating state where individual country operations have local marketing and sales supported by multi-country production and support functions. This development requires, at a minimum, a multi-national organization structure which can evolve to a transnational and even a world enterprise model. In turn, strategy development must be global to ensure that the whole is optimized. However, in Tannahill's viewpoint, an alternative view can be argued. This starts with the premise that the strategy is independent of the global context and that it is the operations plan which takes advantage of, for example, new sourcing opportunities. Globalization becomes a function of the strategy rather than a strategy in its own right.

A company may have a strategic goal to be the world leader in health care. This company would need to take advantage of the synergies afforded by the global business community, but would not have taken advantage of synergies afforded by the global business community in its strategy. Tannahill relates an example in which some industries were in the habit of holding government price negotiation and infrastructure investment discussions more or less in the same breath. The result was overcapacity of production and R&D facilitates worldwide. As governments and industry became more cost-conscious, capacity was reduced to come more into line with demand. However, tough decisions had to be made about where to focus production and research and development facilities and the concept of global sourcing was hatched. The implications to a corporation with global aspiration are unclear as to whether globalization is a strategy in its own right or a means to an end.

In Tannahill's view, the development of strategy exists as a process in which the management of the organization sets the guidelines and constraints outlining the corporation's intent to operate in a global environment. The operating groups within the firm organized either geographically or functionally, by product or by competency must use the guidelines to establish what globalization means relative to local business objectives and the value proposition to its domestic customers. Globalization is not a strategy, but a means to achieve it. Whether you consider globalization to be a strategy or a tactic, the organization needs to be able to think in global terms and embrace a global context. Porter reminds us that, 'Competitive strategy is about being different. It means deliberately choosing a different set of activities to deliver a unique mix of value.'[21]

The essential element in embracing a global context is simply to look beyond the confines of the organization and adopt a worldview placing the business processes, products and services of the firm into a context of one global market. Global strategies are designed with two primary components; motivation and method. Global motivations such as obtaining sale economies, desirable global brand associations, access to low-cost labour or materials, access to national investment incentives, cross-subsidization, dodging trade barriers and access to strategically important markets stem from an internal desire to achieve growth, the arrival of a foreign competitor to your domestic market and/or a direct demand from the existing customer base.[22] The second half of the equation is a method which can be accomplished by adopting an approach to global strategy such as balancing the economies of global standardization versus local desires for customization, forming strategic partnership, developing or linking to an international brand, creating industry collaborations or joint ventures and participation in a network of value to name just a few. To achieve this, an organization must strive to create a common understanding of this global context across the organization. These global views are most effectively communicated by the use of business scenarios, which describe a range of business options based on a specific set of business conditions. It is important to note that scenarios are not predictions of the future nor are they forecasts of business activities, they are possibilities of a business condition that is different than the current business; the scenario may occur at any time in the near or distant future.[23] In order to build a global view or a scenario of a future state it is imperative that organizations develop skills in sensing market conditions and identify trends that will influence the description of future operating states which is the subject of the next section.

Sensing the market, competitors, customers and opportunities

> *Axiom: Market trends shape corporate objectives while customer behaviour shapes organizational goals and business process output.*

Competing in the ever-altering global economy, corporations regardless of industry must be able to sense changes in their customer's behaviour, demand and preferences. To understand the diversity of customer's wants, needs and desires, a company must see their products and services through the eyes of the customer which Day calls market sensing.[24] The inability to sense changes in the marketplace often results in corporations suddenly realizing that a new market entrant has become a threat, or a new product is now revolutionizing the industry in which they operate. In all cases, both the incumbent corporation and the new competitive threat have had access to the same customer bases, so why is threat such a surprise. It would appear that since the corporation already has a relationship with the customer, it should have the advantage and not be surprised with a competitor's offer. Organizations must develop mechanisms that assess continuous alternations in customer needs. Fundamental shifts in consumer demand typically occurs due to three key factors: an attitudinal transformation that takes place over a number of years, such as people's taste changing as they get older, or the shift can be triggered by specific events such as the September 11 catastrophic event which altered many aspects of society, or demand shifts as a result of a technological breakthrough. New levels of competition demands that organizations develop two key corporate competencies; to sense the market and customer behaviour and to establish business processes that adapt to changing customer requirements. Howcroft and Lavis remind us that even companies with a history of successful products fail if they do not innovate their products, sense changes in the customer environment: 'Organizations can become outdated simply because they lack the ability to adapt and conform to the requirements of society.'[25]

From a strategic-thinking perspective, organizations must calculate the consequences of consumer, social and competitive changes relative to the value added by their portfolio products or services. The corporation must first assess if the change is really a long-term alternation in customer behaviour or is the result of a short-term market phenomenon. Changes in customer behaviour demand or preference that happen over long periods often go unnoticed by the firm until after it has already gained sufficient momentum to be noticed such as when a competitor introduces a product to address the new demand. In most firms, this can be attributed to the fact that their attention is often focused on shorter-term revenues and profits. Another key factor is that consumers do not inherently get together and decide to adopt a new behaviour. Corporations that have developed customer-sensing skills are not shocked or surprised when a new market entrant makes an appearance.

To keep abreast of changes in the marketplace, consumer behaviour and the competition corporations do not simply translate into a technological solution. This is where firms often make expensive missteps. Technology, when used effectively, provides valuable information to use in conjunction with other mechanisms such as external data sources and direct customer interactions to be leveraged. The versatility of technology permits a company to experiment and investigate methods to acquire and analyse customer feedback, purchasing behaviour, product effectivity, levels of customer service and other sensing mechanisms. However, Ambler and Styles remind us that understanding customer requirements becomes harder when firms engage in business beyond their local markets.[26]

When corporations engage in both foreign and domestic markets in which highly competitive conditions occur, they minimize opportunities to achieve cost reductions. According to Grime, this is due to a lack of additional mechanisms needed to sense customer behaviour. To reduce cost proactively, a common or centralized infrastructure is needed which can be leveraged across geographically disbursed organizations. Similarly, proactive customer management must use technology to ensure that customer feedback is monitored and acted on quickly. Companies must ensure that all opportunities presented by customers and markets are incorporated into the internal strategic thinking. A firm must implement an infrastructure or engage with partners in a network of values to monitor any opportunities and problems. Grime notes that a way of doing this in lieu of a high-tech approach is by establishing a user group for customers.

In Grime's view, strategy within a company must be made up of the most up-to-date information available, regularly monitored and adjusted according to changes in the marketplace that have direct and sometimes indirect relevance to the firm's value proposition.

The relevance of a new customer's requirements must be considered in accordance to the firm's value proposition under four distinct processes; customer profitability, customer acquisition, customer retention and customer satisfaction.[27] These four processes are at the heart of developing a core competency to sense customers, markets and competitors. Building on this point, Ian Southward, of Fiserv, explains to engage these processes as sensors within the market; strategy itself must move away from a centralized discipline to become more integrated within the business. The company must ensure it builds capabilities to capture, harness and utilize information about its customers, competitors and markets within its people, processes and technology. Southward reminds us that market-sensing processes grow to be valuable to the company only when strategic thinking becomes part of the everyday business of the organization. Market-sensing capabilities are best delivered by harnessing the skills and knowledge of people in the day-to-day roles best positioned to accumulate this information and not a centralized, detached strategy group. Southward provides us with an example: collection of customer information is best captured by sales people and customer service representatives. Information about competitors and market events can be captured by the sales team and marketing teams as well as product development groups.

Here again, Southward considers strategy not as the definition of a future end-state, but as a technique for defining, testing, pursuing, accelerating and abandoning iterative definitions of future end-states. A company must build an iterative-sense and respond-capability that can collect, harness and utilize information in a continually developing series of stages.

Lauren Smith, of Direct Line, reminds us that strategy is only a statement of intended means of achieving objectives, simply a set of long-term preferences, not the objective itself.[28] Therefore, the process of market-sensing strategy development must not only have the capacity to adapt to the changes in the market conditions, but must also adapt to the firm's core competencies or in some cases act to restructure the organization as depicted in Figure 2.6.

In the context of market-sensing strategies, organizations will sense changes in the market or customer, develop a response such as a new product, changes in pricing or additional services and finally they will adapt their business processes to accommodate the new means of adding value. When discussing organizational adaptiveness, Southward puts it this way: 'Even if an organization has built solid processes for monitoring their competition and markets, the first it will know about a change in the market is when a competitor, or new entrant, has already released its new strategy. It takes time for a business to observe

From	To
• Strategy as plan	Strategy as adaptation
• Make-and-buy processes	Sense-and-respond (and sense again) processes
• Isolated 'think tank'	Business value delivery in 3 to 6 month increments
• Hierarchy and bureaucracy	Knowledge and autonomy
• Power as position (power to say 'no')	Power as accountability (power to say 'yes')
• Building a 'City on the Hill'	Building an all-terrain vehicle

Figure 2.6   Shifting the process of strategy

the change, evaluate and consider its response. The politics, culture and processes within an organization can lock it into wide-angled responses that can take time to bring to market.' In a rapidly changing business environment where even Bill Gates stresses that Microsoft is only ever six months away from extinction, today's organizations must build the ability to respond rapidly to competitor and market changes.

For most companies, Milagros Perez-Novoa, of the Cambridge Entrepreneurship Centre, remarks that it is crucial to develop an entrance strategy when introducing a new product or introducing themselves to the market. For this purpose, a feasibility analysis of the market is required. For example, if a bank would like to introduce a new product, that is, an investment fund in the socially responsible investment sector, the strategy of the bank would be based on how to create bank awareness, find out what other banks have the same or similar product, what type of clients they want to reach (followers, innovators, etc.). Regarding competition, they need to know how competitors move in relation to product, price, promotion and place (the 4 Ps).

Alternatively, Anderson and Narus argue that firms should forget the four Ps and opt for an approach based on three-core processes: understanding value, creating value and delivering value.[29] In their view, a market-sensing process first collects information and in turn generates knowledge to influence decision making, next the process must create and more importantly manage new products or services, augmenting them to construct market offerings while bringing them to market, finally, they must assess the level of fulfilment between customer requirements and supplier offerings to achieve customer satisfaction.

In either case, companies must use market/customer-sensing mechanisms as an integral component of learning which responds to new demands and requirements. The process of learning customer and market behaviour must be based on rapidly assessing the relevance of information while assessing the capabilities of the organization to deliver to the new customer criteria.

Perez-Novoa relates such an example in the learner between the Halifax Bank of Scotland (HBOS) and Clerical Medical in August 2002, when offering narrowly focused products and services to both customers and employees. HBOS realized that to deliver cooperative products or services the essential first step is to educate the employees on the product's applicability to their everyday life situation. Having identified with the product the employees in turn become the best sales people to external customers. Since the products were focused on a specific market segment the internal strategy was to engage employees to closely monitor the demand curve to address issues such as market timing, market conditions, pricing and competitive offerings.

Building on Perez-Novoa's point, Smith claims that business over time tends to become so close to their markets, competitors and consumers, that it is very difficult to stop the 'bumping' and take a genuine step back from the detail. The process of stepping back to take a strategic look at the business conditions can be accomplished using a variety of techniques such as employing external research sources which we will discuss later in this chapter, and engaging a process of scenario planning. A scenario-planning process which proves satisfying (it certainly provoked insight, though it will play out in the future as to whether it was 'successful') begins in some cases by non product-specific research teams. By starting the initial phases using people who had no in-depth 'business bias' the process of scenario planning aims at not missing aspects which might impact the business in unexpected ways.

Smith puts it this way, an initial PESTEL analysis looks at Political, Economic, Social, Technological, Environmental and Legal (or regulatory) arenas. By splitting the research aspects, each researcher becomes close to his/her area and passionate about getting his/her identified trends put on the agenda for consideration. Past and current trends are detailed in conjunction with future forecasts of trends also documented. Smith emphasizes the wealth of future-looking information on the Internet ranging from government forecasts to independent futurists eager to share their observations. However, when using the Internet as a source for information, it is always prudent to verify the source of data due to the increasing amount of unsubstantiated and baseless information that can be found from sources that employ fewer rigours in their methods. This is an important factor when considering data from the Internet because in many cases surveys often do not readily disclose corollary data of such a sample size and demographic mix.

Smith continues to explain that a scenario-planning workshop typically examines each trend and generates upward of 50+ hypotheses based on various trends (e.g. the ageing of the population will continue). During the course of this type of method, the Executive team is involved at regular intervals with the workshop to rank the hypotheses according to likelihood and potential impact on the business. As an iterative process, the more significant hypotheses are bundled into five key scenarios, reflecting on issues about consumer behaviour in the future, the potential technologies in our business to the changing nature of our competitive landscape. This allows for the consideration of strategic actions or responses to each scenario and in the very least focuses management thinking within a process to substantiate the solution to each scenario.

Management teams will always favour scenarios that are comfortable offering less risk and early returns, which seemingly represent a tactical agenda. This is to be expected, though the imminently tangible should not be the only scenarios, which are kept on the corporate radar screen. Whilst focusing on the high-profile scenarios and planning for their eventuality, many of the other 'discarded' hypotheses should remain within the remit of the strategic thinkers to keep an active watching brief. The resultant themes from any scenario exercise are not surprising. The gravity often comes with the realization that certain trends have escalated in such a way in the last five years that if the projection continues to hold, essential business actions need to begin now. The works of Rohit Talwar and his contemporaries fuel the imagination but a word of warning with timescales. Scenario planning is undoubtedly a very interesting activity, but they sometimes look too far ahead (perhaps beyond 5–10 years) and the participants quickly polarize into two types: those who just cannot imagine that far, and those who cannot reign themselves in from the 20-year and beyond horizon.

Perez-Novoa and Smith both make good points: that scenario-based planning must contain two key elements: relevance to both the current and future business conditions, while providing an approach to achieving the operating conditions of the scenarios planned state of business execution. In all cases, scenario planning must provide a vision of future operating conditions and an approach, not a solution to arrive at the desired scenario. Scenario planning breaks down when it attempts to project too far into the future, in many cases, beyond the team's collective belief of any combination of trends. For example, looking back at the last five years of technology evolution one can project (not predict) the next generation of technological uses; it seems impossible to predict how technology will evolve during the next 20 years. However, the applied use of technology to drive business value can be projected two, five or even ten years based on historical behaviour. That is to say although it is difficult to predict the capabilities and features that technology may possess in the future, how corporations will use technology is predictable: to increase access to markets, to reduce operating cost, to improve customer service, to collaborate with other enterprises and various other activities. Scenario development must be based on the establishment of specific operating principles to which the strategy becomes a mechanism for achieving an operating state to support those principles as demonstrated in the following case study.

Case study: Michigan Library Consortium In 1998, the staff of the Michigan Library Consortium and its executive board applied the process of scenario building to change the way in which they viewed future activities of the consortium. The group realized that the foundation for scenario development was to develop a clear and precise understanding of the core values and strategic purposes:[30]

Core values
- Maintaining our integrity, creating and sharing trust and practising ethical behaviour.
- Quality and excellence in our products and our services.
- Adding value through cooperation (in all ways including economic, facilitation, technology, citizenship, service and leadership).
- Leadership and innovation within the Michigan Library Community (MLC).
- Encourage individual growth through an open and participative work environment.

Strategic purposes
- Helping librarians in the State of Michigan fulfil the information needs of their patrons and users with information technology.
- Bringing the resources of individual libraries together in order to maximize their impact, provide cost-and-time benefits, and make the availability of professional knowledge and expertise accessible and affordable.
- To build, serve and provide leadership to the statewide library community.
- To improve the overall level of library service in the state using information technology.

- Keeping libraries relevant through the coordination of information and activities, seeking out the best products and services, and presenting it in a user-friendly format.
- Serving an educational role; providing training, gathering and distributing information, and ensuring that MLC's offerings and benefits are well known and understood.

In MLC's case, the core values and strategic purposes provide not the end-state of the organization's vision but establish the boundaries in which it will achieve its goals and objectives. The consortium's approach sets forth a strategic framework in which individuals can gauge their individual actions and decisions against a specific set of qualified strategic intentions.

Using scenario planning as one approach to strategy development, James Leaton-Gray, from the BBC, reminds us that strategy is not a fixed thing. However brilliant a ten-year plan is, it can be out of date ten days into its life. The strategic organization has to maintain its strategic plan constantly. As the environment changes so must the strategy. This cannot, and should not, mean that the organization is constantly holding strategic away-days and indulges in enforced navel gazing, it does however mean that mechanisms must be in place to update and revise the overall plan as the world moves around you.

Leaton-Gray makes his point very well and advises teams to set parameters for their most significant environmental influences to manage the expectations on the pace of change you expect in your environment. If the real world moves outside those boundaries, the higher pace of external change triggers a review of the strategy. The process of setting the limits is of itself useful because it challenges you to define the environment for which your strategy has been created. If a review is being triggered too frequently, you need to decide whether it is because you have set your parameters too narrowly, is your environment really changing that fast or is your view of it too nervous, then your plan is not flexible enough. Alternatively, in Leaton-Gray's view, you may be measuring the need for tactical manoeuvres and not strategic change. Teams should ask themselves, is your plan truly strategic, or a description of tactical actions? Tactics are just as important as strategy, but they do not need to appear in strategic plans.

Corporations must be cognizant of the influence of changes in the business environment or shifts in the economic climate on the strategic objectives of the firm. These factors compound an organization's ability to achieve long-term goals and objectives because if the pace of external change is too faster than the rate at which the firm re-evaluates its strategic objectives the firm will in effect never reach its goals. If trigger points within a strategic plan are never reached, should you leave the plan gathering dust on the CEO's shelf? Clearly not, according to Leaton-Gray, in the past a map sufficed as an aid to navigation, if you were in unfamiliar territory it provided clues to your whereabouts and could guide you along your route, steering you clear of dangers. Now, however, you can use a hand-held global positioning system (GPS) device, allowing it to update constantly your position with unparalleled accuracy. The strategic plan should be a mobile and ever-changing guide to your business position. It should not be a document like a map, finished and thereafter unchanged, it needs to be receiving information all the time and building and rebuilding your understanding of where you are, and where you are going.

The problem of a continuously updated strategic plan is that organizations use it to make a dangerous transition to a means to act simply on tactical situations or current problem states. This raises the question of how we can constantly update the strategic plan without our business slowly stopping? Leaton-Gray continues to explain: the word sensing in the title of this section is very important. In business a 'hunch' is viewed in the same way as it is in classic police-based drama, senior people are suspicious of it. But, like the maverick cop in the drama, a good employee's hunch may be closer to the truth than any number of consultant-led number-based market analyses. The human being is the most complex computer available to your firm, allow it to process as it sees fit. When one of your 'old lags' announces that he senses that something is happening to his customers, take the time to investigate. If you wish to give this process of sensing a title, call it Knowledge Management, but do not underestimate the importance of the market information locked away in the minds of your experienced staff.

The process of continuously or periodically evaluating business conditions as a means to re-evaluate the long-term objectives of the firm is tenuous for most firms because it requires processing information from many sources against the current conditions within the context of today's business activities. To many firms, this process is best accomplished using one of two methods: utilizing external resources such as academics, research firms or specialty consultants, or establishing a capability within the firm that lines of business can use as a resource for objective thinking. In larger organizations, a combination of both methods may be required to provide intelligence for global or transnational product lines and services.

Corporations that use external resources such as academics, research firms or specialty consultants have recently been disillusioned by the inability of these groups to forecast the future in the wake of the dot-com era. However, the value of an external view is critical to the long-term success of the organization and must be considered a strategic resource in and of itself, because it is not cost effective for the company to be looking at all things at all times. Simply the corporation does not have the resources to monitor the scope of the global business environment coupled with the pace at which competitive change is occurring. Therefore, acquiring an external view of the markets, competitors, customers and the firm itself is a critical input in the formulation of strategy. Alan Whitaker puts it this way when discussing why firms use future trends analysts in successful strategic planning, because of not knowing what lies ahead, relying only on gut feeling or limited knowledge of senior management can lead to two different types of failure.

Failing to choose the right wave

Whitaker, who is a surfer, describes it this way: 'I have spent countless hours sitting on my surfboard with my back to the beach scouring the horizon for the perfect wave. Big waves come in sets, with several minutes between sets. Even when a highly "surfable" wave arrives, most surfers wait believing that later waves will be even bigger, but most times they are not and the opportunity is missed.' Corporations use future trends analysts, to better recognize the right time to enter or leave a market to launch a new product or initiative. Too soon or too late is always extremely costly and damaging to the reputation of senior executives and the morale of the company. The use of these external sources enables the firm to fine tune market timings, product designs and other competitive advantages.

Whitaker continues to explain: 'when a surfer identifies the "right" wave, he/she will paddle over to the expected point which will provide the greatest lift and velocity as it breaks. The surfer turns the board to face the shore and begins to paddle forward waiting for the unbroken wave to pick them up and propel them forward. If they are too close to the beach, they will "wipe out" with the wave, which will break on top of them, pushing them to the ocean floor. A few yards too back means they will miss the target take off and be left behind.' Corporations use future trends analysts as ready resources to contribute to the new process of strategic planning within line organizations as they prepare to launch new products and initiatives. Companies that are now engaged in the process of aggregating strategic thinking across the firm must look beyond the 'waves' they can see still approaching them. Often firms are so pre-occupied with trying to beat competitors in our own industry, we fail to take account of other developments that could wipe us out in a few months. Here Whitaker relates such an example: 'when I was at high school, I remember the battle between dry cleaners. As they continually invested in the latest technology, they were able to offer ever-quicker service. First, I remember "In today, back tomorrow". Then "In by eight back by five", later "in by nine out by four". Even later, "In by ten out by two". But they did not recognise the development of wash and wear clothing until it was too late. Within a year, about 80% of the dry cleaners in the area I lived had closed down.'

The primary value in utilizing external sources is not to seek answers but to establish dialogues within the company that are future looking. The most significant contribution of these external sources is not the prognostication of the future state of business but the generation of questions within the firm to challenge our current thinking. The objective is to gain a combined picture of the future, which can be translated into a new operating state for the long-term viability of the firm and its products or services.

Organizations such as Skandia have adopted an approach that established Skandia Future Centers consisting of a global team of 30 people that form five Future Teams with a mission: to explore five key driving forces of the business environment – the European insurance market, demographics, technology, the world economy, organization and leadership.[31] The Skandia team's goal is to present a vision of the company's future to the corporate council of 150 senior executives. The Future Teams model is built on deliberately mixing generations (junior employees to senior executives) functional roles, organizational experiences and cultural backgrounds with the explicit intent of creating intellectual capital from the dialogues that occur both within the teams and from the interactions of the teams with the firm.

Another example is Siemens Nixdorf Information Systems FutureScape Team, which employs younger people throughout the firm to challenge the board of directors and the corporate strategies by using a process that engages the team to look beyond today's boundaries to reshape the firm's thinking about markets, products, technology and social change.[32] Porter makes a critical observation pointing out that external factors act to alter a company's strategy, as factors within the organization often act consciously or unconsciously to dismantle the effectivity of strategic initiatives or simply cause strategies to fail: 'A sound strategy is undermined by a misguided view of competition, by organizational failures, and, especially, by the desire to grow.'[33] The difficulty of the internalizing of strategy is the topic to which we now turn.

3
Developing the Strategic Corporate Competency

One of the issues discussed by the practitioners was why some companies are simply better at strategy development and execution than others. One could argue that the main culprit of a firm's strategic failures is an inherent misunderstanding of companies' competencies, capabilities, talent and abilities. Day makes an important point in that the most effective strategies are the result of management initiating a challenge to which business teams must think broadly to look for improvement or innovation.[34] In Day's view, the adaptive strategies or the process of adaptive planning often forces changes in managerial roles requiring traditional corporate strategies to become facilitators of the process or integrators.

This raises the question of how an organization takes a geographically dispersed set of capable individuals and creates a strategic competency. Corporations can establish core competencies in strategy when they focus the process of strategy development on building fewer concepts or a limited number of initiatives.[35] This concentration of resources when taken together provides organizational cohesion, balance and boundaries for the coordination of geographically dispersed resources. However, firms in a transition between operating states tend to overmanage the development of strategies across the organizational hierarchy. To reduce the tendency of the organization to erect barriers to any process, strategy development alone is not enough; managers must take on a new role that of process facilitator and jettison their traditional role acting as control point for approval. Loveridge makes an important point that the organization will naturally establish boundaries as resources are applied to any process: 'Within most large organizations internal boundaries grow up around "communities of practice" created by daily interactions in specialized tasks.'[36]

To take a more parochial or academic view, Chaffee considers three contrasting views to strategy: linear strategy adaptive strategy and interpretive strategy.[37] Taking a linear approach to strategy development can be found in most large organizations who engage in a process of planning and forecasting. Hammer reminds us that within many corporations the formalized process of planning and forecasting is not strategic planning and over time evolves into a ritualistic budget exercise with projections that resemble fortune telling.[38] Corporations which employ an adaptive approach to strategy place an emphasis on fitting or considering the means of the firm as a focus of management's attention. Few companies have stepped up to the challenge of considering an interpretive model of strategy as a metaphor which cannot be measured quantitatively and must be considered in qualitative terms.

One new direction in strategy that did not surface during our discussions on strategy but must also be reviewed by corporations is the IBM's SMASH concept. IBM's new approach to how computers should function is predicated on a three-part formula: simple, many, self-healing. These three components, which have been labelled as autonomic computing, merge strategy and implementation using an almost biological approach to strategy and execution. The concept that was originally developed as a model for computing can be applied to the process and execution of corporate strategies and business operations in general. Fishman noted the application of the model by imagining a firm with no all-controlling central brain and no separation between thinkers and doers where the information on the transactions within the business are guide to the behaviour of the firm's resources.[39] Within IBM's autonomic-computing manifesto are eight key principles that are the fundamental elements of strategy development required for today's competitive environment:[40]

- *Know thyself – possess identity*: people within large organizations must be more aware of the full capabilities of the firm, how those capabilities can be utilized or borrowed and the limits to what can be shared or isolated. In large organizations, it is common for groups to work on similar or identical problems unaware of others within the firm tackling the same problem.
- *Configure and reconfigure under varying and unpredictable conditions*: organizations must become increasingly flexible in their application of resources to changing global business conditions. However, the interval between stopping one activity and reorganizing for a new activity represents lost time, additional cost and missed opportunity.

- *Always look to optimize its workings*: self-optimization is the only means to compete under the conditions of a dynamic business climate, maintaining the status quo is no longer a viable alternative for business. Organizations must establish comprehensive internal and external mechanisms of feedback to assess continually their ability to deliver to customers, suppliers and employees.

- *Recover from routine and extraordinary events that cause failure in parts*: problem resolution must be delegated down to the level within the organization that is closest to the problem. As problems escalate within the firm they consume greater amounts of resources to resolve, at each level of escalation the inertia gathered by the consumption of resources reduces the amount of resources on hand to conduct the normal aspects of the business, solve other problems and address customer demands.

- *Self-protection*: the organization must sense intrusions and other compromises ranging from physical and virtual security to intellectual and customer centric loss. Protecting the firm from physical and electronic harm is a given. Corporations must also consider protecting intellectual property especially when they compete based on a proprietary process or unique knowledge, much of which can be loss or eroded by outsourcing contracts or during times of high-employee turnover.

- *Know its environment and the context surrounding its activities, and act accordingly*: as corporations become more like cooperating cells of corporate competencies, the need to understand what they do in the context of their markets, increases their ability to sense changes and develop responses. Corporations, regardless of market conditions, must maintain their reliability for customers and develop an ability to adapt their products and services based on knowledge aggregated across the firm on the context of transactions initiated by customers. Corporations must learn how to interact with other firms simply and economically under multiple sets of rules governing their interoperating behaviour.

- *Cannot exist in a hermitic environment*: without compromising its ability to manage independently on itself, a firm must learn to operate in a heterogeneous world of business, because it is no longer insulated by the rules within one domestic or single foreign marketplace. Corporations must now think transnationally and learn how to coexist in a global marketplace. More importantly, corporations have to develop new skills that enable them to leverage an increasing interdependence on firms when they serve customers that are beyond their traditional markets.

- *Anticipate the optimized resources needed and keep the complexity hidden from customer:* as corporations merge, acquire, partner, affiliate and become more intertwined in their day-to-day activities it is imperative not to alienate customers during the process of redirecting resources.

IBM's model is important to business strategy because it provides a ready framework in which all strategies can be built addressing the eight fundamental areas of business concerns. More importantly, it is a litmus test for existing strategies to measure the extent of their approach in addressing these business issues. As a framework in which to build a foundation for strategy development, the IBM approach reduces the amount of corporate strategy fragmentation or multiple strategies working at cross-purposes competing for the same resources.

The IBM framework supports Porter's view, which argues that companies that try almost anything or everything lack a cohesive strategy. The true art to strategy is setting limits to what is to be accomplished while considering the fact that the company cannot operate thinking that it can simply do what its competitors do, only better, for any extending period by betting on the incompetence of its competitors.[41] One could argue that this has been the posture of business since the dot-com collapse, now focusing almost exclusively on increasing operational effectiveness. Ultimately, a strategy of incremental improvement is no strategy at all. It ends up placing the firm in a competitive downward spiral. Porter makes this point clear: 'Continuous incremental improvement is not a strategy. Neither is imitating and emulating competitors. When rivals offer most (if not all) of the same product varieties, features, and services, employ the same distribution channels and match one another's production process, none has a distinct competitive advantage.'[42] Unlike many eCommerce futurists, Porter was one of the few voices (sometimes a lone voice) during the dot-com era relentlessly advocating that the electronically enabled changing business climate did not suddenly invalidate the laws of economics.[43]

As businesses and their supporting business processes become increasingly interdependent and connected via computers and telecommunications, technology becomes an invisible silent servant similar to the mature technology of electricity, which we notice only when it fails. This inter-intra-extra operating state of the firm must be built on a framework like IBM's autonomous computing model simply because it provides the firm with two distinct strategic elements; a discipline or rigour in the formation of strategies and a comprehensiveness which will enable firms to achieve a higher degree of aggregated cross-organizational strategic thinking. The first step in applying a framework such as the autonomous computing model is to develop capabilities that sense changes in the firm's operating environment, which is the subject of the next section.

Anticipating the competition and understanding market trends

> *Axiom: To anticipate market behaviour and resolve the ambiguities of strategy a process of projecting what is known must be used, not predicting what might be.*

Competition is not simply outwitting every other provider of a product or service that your firm offers to the market. Competitive strategies centre on knowing how to anticipate changes in the market's behaviour and time the actions of the firm to meet the new levels of demand. Most organizations plan for increases in demand; few corporations plan for anticipated downturns; even fewer plan for a product or service to retirement leaving a customer's transition from one product to the next simply to an assumption that the customer will sort out the process. Few products last forever. From a strategic perspective, all product or service plans should address the creation, development, production and ultimate retirement of each customer offering. Anticipating the competition is not forecasting demand, clairvoyance or magic; it is simply understanding data and realizing a trend. Market and customer trends occur at three distinct levels: micro, intermediate and macro.

Identifying customer trends and competitive reactions is the mainstay of the micro-level area of understanding. Recognizing the relationships between market pricing, costs, transaction volumes and other front line activities is a vital input to the formation of strategies. However, the sheer volume of information at this level makes it imperative that corporations devise information filtering mechanisms to summarize, collate and prioritize the actions of customer behaviour and other market patterns to separate anomalies from true trends.

The intermediate-level of trends analysis centres on understanding trends and factors that influence the direction of the firm and/or its participation in a network of value. Analysts must apply principles such as the Heckscher–Ohlin factor proportions theory,[44] product lifecycle, customer preference analysis, Edgeworth box[45] and other analytical tools to determine the potential impact of a rising trend to the entirety of the firm's business activities.

At the macro-level, trends must be understood in relation to the whole market or in context to the market sub-segments to which they have a direct influence. Analyses at the macro-level must seek out and identify determinants of the market such as the adoption rate of new technology by society where one society embraces the innovation more rapidly than another as witnessed in the mobile phone marketplace.

Jane Roe of Corven carries the opinion that most companies are inclined to follow the competition and tend to adopt a sheep-like mentality, ultimately misreading the market all together. The truly great CEO has the fortitude to be the first to do something and benefits from 'first mover advantage'. The difficult part is to know what to do first. Clearly, a thorough analysis of the competition, customers and of the environment is important, but in many organizations, the analysis becomes mechanical, making or jettisoning true insight because it challenges the status quo. Organizations that have subscribed to this process often suffer from analysis paralysis. Real groundbreaking moves tend to rely more on instinct and emotion than on analysis, since analysis tends to be historical and backward looking.

Case study: Yorkshire Electricity   Roe puts this into context by elaborating with a case study from the utility industry. Since privatization, utilities have been struggling to improve profitability whilst maintaining an aging network infrastructure. They have typically been plagued by poor labour relations, low productivity and inadequate controls and transparency of costs. The manager of Yorkshire Electricity's asset maintenance department recognized an opportunity to address this challenge in what was then a novel and innovative way. Through a management buyout he negotiated the transfer of Yorkshire Electricity's direct labour force (those field staff working on network maintenance and repairs) to a new company, which he set up, called Freedom. However, instead of these staff becoming employees of Freedom, they were established either individually or in small groups, as franchises. Freedom provided the central support and necessary training, whilst former employees became self-employed. Freedom was given the contract to carry out maintenance and repairs for Yorkshire Electricity, who only paid agreed rates for specific jobs completed – they enjoyed better value for money with fixed costs becoming variable. The franchises were motivated to get through as many jobs as possible, since they were only paid for jobs completed. Freedom subsequently won contracts with a number of other utilities including Yorkshire water, 24Seven, East

Midlands Electricity and has now expanded beyond utilities into other sectors. In a few short years, they have grown to a business with a turnover of £100 million.

An implication of Yorkshire Electricity's strategy according to Roe is that the founder of Freedom did not consider whether the franchise model to outsource utility maintenance had been done before or was proven. He had a passion for what he was setting up and believed in its benefits not just to potential customers (utilities) but also to employees. No amount of analysis can substitute for having a passion for what you are doing and this passion frequently only comes when you are the first to do something. Roe notes that business leaders tend to have been through rigorous training such as MBA programmes. This tends to stifle one's ability to follow gut instinct since there is a tendency to want to follow a rigorous process of analysis to reduce risk, before making any 'moves'. It is difficult to prove that a concept will be successful in the future by historical analysis and forward-looking analysis is inevitably inaccurate.

Case study: career management   Lloyd builds on Roe's observation with another case study based on his personal experience while working as a civil engineer in various delightful tropical paradises. Lloyd progressively realized that the development projects on which he was engaged did not appear to proceed according to the careful planning which had been done (often years earlier, at the time that the application for aid funding had been initiated). With diligent out-of-hours covert research in dining rooms and bars, he realized that in spite of everyone's attempts to portray life as following the plan, this was in fact the norm and happening with everybody else's projects too. Lloyd saw that engineers kept on encountering problems in their projects and kept on devising ingenious technical solutions. But in fact these problems frequently shared a common theme: there were people behaving in 'illogical' ways; A skilled driver writing off an expensive grader by driving it over the edge of a high embankment while drunk; farmers being unable to agree on how to share water from an irrigation outlet, so that there were those that could overwater their land, while downstream farmers suffered from drought; bureaucrats delaying importation of an essential vehicle for a famine relief team; and so many more. To Lloyd's surprise, he realized that although his degree and professional qualification had failed to teach him about these issues, they were in fact the determinants of a successful project. Not only had Lloyd not been trained in these human problems, but nor had his technical colleagues and in most cases they had not even recognized that they were not technical problems. Candidly, Lloyd remarks that he had always found that the most technical parts of his engineering and economics degree provided little stimulus as a sense of personal accomplishment so he decided to carve a career as the interface between people and technology: training, communication, management, operations and maintenance. Lloyd acknowledges that even now the appropriate term 'terotechnology' is unrecognized and never used.

Case study: parenting   Lloyd offers a very pragmatic case study; parents have a difficult role when attempting to impose their strategic vision on their children. All too often, it leads to rejection, alienation and other counterproductive results. Nevertheless, Lloyd has always regarded parenting as the most pervasive (and therefore under-recognized) management development experience on offer. The skills of communication and influence, time and resource management, budgeting and planning, that we learn and practise as a parent are equally applicable (suitably disguised and unacknowledged: colleagues do not enjoy being told that they are behaving just like their three-year old) in the workplace.

From a strategic advantage point, Lloyd offers two examples from his personal experience. It will not surprise the reader to hear that he has been influenced in his choice of city (Cambridge) and home by considerations of his daughters' upbringing and education: where will they go to school, who will their school fellows and neighbours be. These are strategic considerations: it is ensuring that one is in the right place at the right time, maximizing the probability for the right opportunities to arise, even though one cannot predict precisely what shape they will take and when they will occur. Amongst the many benefits, there are a circle of exceptionally talented friends who have also acted as encouragements to try harder and benchmarks of achievable performance, attendance at an outstanding dance school which gave theatrical opportunities as well as coordination, exercise, a love for dance and music, many first-rate teachers and mentors, a musical education that has included learning to play the harp (definitely a minority instrument outside Wales, and therefore a source of great comparative advantage) and singing in choirs.

Lloyd consciously tried in the 1980s to influence his daughter to study German, as he perceived that it was a language spoken by a very large number of Europeans (100 million East and West Germans, Swiss, Austrians) with exceptional economic influence and great cultural richness, and yet was spoken by remarkably few British people. She duly complied and did the German option at school, did work experience in a Hamburg court, and even studied German as a specialist subject at

Advanced Level. Lloyd suspected and achieved compliance at the expense of ownership: his daughter did not enjoy it, did not perform as well as her ability would have ensured in another subject and has not pursued an interest in German language or culture. In this case, Lloyd identified and anticipated a long-range trend that from a strategic career development perspective, acquiring a proficiency in German is an essential component of a well-balanced pallet of skills required to compete in a future job market. However, his daughter was neither stimulated by the environment and work, nor did she aspire to the same career options as her father, which is not surprising to most parents. The point that Lloyd makes with his personal story is the best way to anticipate long-term trends and develop corresponding strategies by engaging in a bidirectional dialogue which identifies the objectives and formulates an approach together. This is at the heart of most strategic failures in business, that is, when the strategy is viewed as a mandate form of management having been derived from little or no dialogue.

Case study: Formul 1 Hotel   Dembitz provides us with a view of how anticipating the marketplace can be as simple as listening to customers as he describes the process in which Formul 1 Hotel undertook the most exhaustive market analysis, and analysis of user requirements. They discovered that what the vast majority of business travellers required was a fast and efficient registration and check out process, relatively comfortable and spacious rooms with excellent beds and bathroom facilities (all normally associated with three star or plus hotels), but they did not require restaurants, bars, room service, concierge, newspapers and other such services. A new hotel model was therefore created catering specifically for the identified market. The hotel was fully automated; credit card swipe-based access and checkout – just like the airlines have now established – offers three-star comfort, without any service, at one-star pricing. The model has proven to be a huge success, and has now been emulated by others; however, Formul 1 Hotel has carved a good slice of the market for itself.

As individuals within business units take action, their efforts in converting strategic initiatives to tactical actions are for the most part, wholly successful, partially successful or disastrous. In each case, information on the outcomes from these activities originating at the front lines of business provide valuable data which must be used as input into subsequent iterations of strategy formulation. One could argue that, in many cases, organizations learn more about the execution of strategy through a series of failures than by a string of successful strategy implementations because failures identify and test the limitations of the firm in ways that establish boundaries on the application of resources and how strategy and action should mutually inform.

Learning by doing

In Bradley's view a failed strategy is not always the product of poor management (although in some cases it may be); they are instead opportunities to understand the limits of the firm's resources, capabilities and corporate competencies. These strategic misinterpretations are often attributed to breakdowns in communications, expectations or simply lack of committed resources to perform effectively the associated tasks. Figure 3.1 illustrates a key point that the development of a corporate competency in dynamic strategy development is a process enriched by learning by doing. The key to the philosophy of this approach is that strategic initiatives should be constructed in such a way that they can become modular components when they are deconstructed into tactical actions. This modularity limits potential damage such as the loss of invested capital, misapplied intellectual capital and other misalignment of resources. The point that Bradley makes is that no organization can get strategic implementation right every time, therefore, the firm must learn to fail fast and in small iterative steps to minimize potential collateral damage to other strategic initiatives. This becomes a paramount concern when strategic initiatives cross organizations and/or cross partnerships in a network of value.

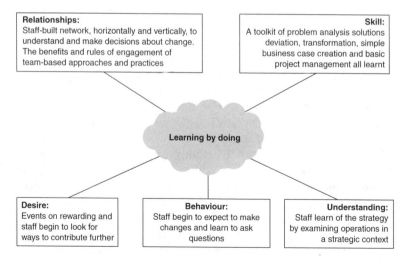

Figure 3.1 The 'Learning by doing' graphic

Devising strategy collaboratively

> *Axiom: Collaboration is a process that fundamentally acts as a relationship with a lifecycle.*

Collaboration, co-opetition and cooperation are rapidly becoming not merely business options, but a way of life to compete in the global environment. Collaboration on a strategic level occurs in one of three ways: *intra-organizational, inter-organizational* such as strategic alliances based on competitive and cooperative intent found within a partnership,[46] and *extra-organizational*, which Nalebuff and Brandenburger labelled 'co-opetition'.[47] In all cases, collaboration must be based on the generation of value as a product of combining the resources of two or more organizational competencies in a relationship that forms a symbiosis. Relationships that do not achieve a symbiotic relationship in which the success of each party is dependent on the combined efforts of both reflect a simple supplier relationship. Collaborative strategies share risks and rewards. Parker relates to us that it is important when disseminating the details of strategy to understand that different viewpoints will need to be accommodated. For example, as a training course in a computer manufacturing company, this was illustrated when the workings of an integrated circuit were presented to the software and hardware engineers at the same time. The hardware engineer wanted to know how the voltage change on one pin would affect the output on a second pin if the voltage was either constant or varied on a third pin. The software engineers, on the other hand, wished to understand the process whereby a logical change would affect the result depending upon time-varied sequences. Parker realized that both parties were asking the same question, but in their own language.

Parker makes an important point that is illustrated in Figure 3.2, that strategies must be described to operating groups within the firm in a manner, which is understood, by the group.

Smith further refines Parker's observations by acknowledging that viewpoints must be considered throughout the process of strategy development, execution and the collection of feedback; in essence, all communications regarding a strategy must strive to be in a form understandable to each subgroup within the organization. In Smith's viewpoint, although the initial foundation of the high-level strategic direction is often discussed by a small team of executives, most strategists will heartily agree that the more people involved and bought in to the strategic action plans and initiatives, the more advocates within the

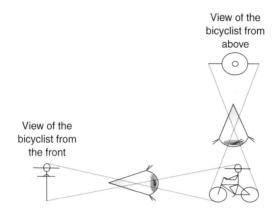

Figure 3.2 Viewpoints on the same subject

business to make it a success. 'The wider variety of perspectives involved the more insightful the resultant strategy is likely to emerge' is a little less easy to swallow, when it necessitates the engagement and real involvement of non-senior management. On a variety of levels, the workforce at large can be capitalized upon for an alternative perspective often lacking in the focused Management Team, as described in the following examples:

1 Consumer research groups (of employees) looking at new product or service propositions (let us not forget we are all consumers) and giving their views before expensive research is commissioned can be a wise additional activity to the product development process. At the later stage, new products can where applicable be softly launched to employees as a trial package – a sure fire way to highlight any gaps in service standards before the product is open to marketplace scrutiny and the brand substantially at risk.

2 Where front line staff can be involved, product-specific workshops can be invaluable in highlighting where customers lack understanding, are pleased or dissatisfied with current products or even make comments and comparisons with competitor offerings. As the people who speak to the customers every day, it is logical but often overlooked to ask employees to represent the customer voice.

3 Workout sessions: intensive workshops based on all scales of process improvement and gaining efficiencies in the business have proved very successful in a number of companies. Often by resolving to iron out smaller inefficiencies in the processes within the back office of

the business these quick fixes can lead to bigger benefits than expected.

These activities according to Smith can form work-streams of strategic initiatives in process redesign or product development, while also highlighting issues that may need to be addressed by action plans going forward. In this way, the strategic input can filter back towards the high-level strategic plan and continually shape the detail of this working document. This level of strategic engagement provides far more benefits than those that can be put on the cost-benefit analysis. By involving the front line staff in the strategic planning process in this way a more committed and loyal employee base can emerge. Making clear that the workforce are valued and can help the business in a wider sense than achieving weekly key performance indicators (KPIs) is an incredibly motivating force.

The change in expectations

Changing social expectations, consistent with a new era of consciousness, increasingly triggering questions such as what could I be doing, what should I be doing enabled by a progressively richer, more stable and socially more caring environment? Senior managers continually struggling with how they can continue to drive shareholder returns and are now realizing – or maybe just hoping – that the much valued latent talent of the broader organization might be the source of the new ideas that could drive product and service innovation, drive new level of financial performance and define new and distinct operating models. Whether business drivers are born out of short-term desperation or a genuine belief that only a new business model based on a renew contract between management and staff will continue to drive the returns that have enabled us to arrive at this point in our evolution. The reality is that the expectations of both management and staff are changing the result of which could be the basis of a new explicit working and social contract. Will collaboration make this possible? Corporations operating in the global economy consider three key areas when devising their collaborative strategies: *leadership, trust* and *training*.

A new leadership model

First, organizations must recognize a fundamental change in how leaders lead which is redefining the nature of leadership. Leadership can be found at all levels with the organization and not just at the top, but regardless of where an individual may find themselves there are a number of principles/characteristics:

- *Vision and tenacity*: maintaining your belief in the ability of someone to make a real difference and in the face of difficulties/early failures do not revert to classical models of problem solving.
- *Humility*: be willing to have your ideas subsumed without feeling the need to be right or to be in control.
- *Manage discomfort and ambiguity but do not take the bait*: collaborative strategy formulation can seem chaotic and non-linear unlike technical strategy approaches, key is that senior management are able to push the accountability back down to those involved without taking the bait and looking for the easy way out. Once the bait is seen as having been taken, a new protocol has been established that will be very difficult to reverse.
- *Manage the tension within the system*: a new model will bring new tensions at all levels, staff will find the challenges unsettling, middle management will question their role and can react in more heavy-handed fashion, senior leaders can feel a lack of control and find it very easy to revert to more comfortable management styles.
- *Daily demonstration of action consistent with the collaboration*: at all levels leaders need on a daily basis to be able to point to something that they have done consistent with what has been stated.
- *Continual communication of the business vision and the chosen strategies for delivering on it*: helping in a 'Darwin' fashion the strategic thinking to evolve and broaden at all levels within the thinking.

Creating a trusting environment

Second, corporate cynism is rising; pension scandals, exorbitant executive pay packages, lack of coherence between performance and reward, the increasing militancy of unions and their leadership makes this the most challenging of the three areas to address. Areas to be targeted include:

- Re-establishing a sense of a single corporate identity, not staff and management or finance versus HR or France versus United Kingdom or product A versus product B, and so on. Requires a unifying vision and a common purpose. Creates a lens that individuals can look through that informs their action without the need for process, bureaucracy and hierarchy.
- Foster programmes that drive and enable collaborative learning, redefining who you can learn from, fostering new networks and putting the organization back in touch with itself.

• Create forums that legitimize the challenge and questioning of all staff (see the following discussion on approaches Fishbowls, W-O, Labs, Contracting, etc.).

• Defining a 'new' contract with staff based on a commitment of keeping the organization informed, engaged and highly employable.

Developing the collaborative strategy gym and training programme

Third, collaborative strategy is unknown to most; those who are aware of it may see it as highly risky and the controlled nature of more technical approaches to strategy may appeal, regardless of one's starting point. To most this will represent a new and challenging shift in thinking that individuals need to train for and de-risk before embarking. You might be a great 100 m sprinter but to run a marathon there needs to be a very different training regime. Building the collaborative strategy muscle needs to be measured if you are not to injure yourself or put off the rest of the organization.

There are two distinct set of tools: those focused on large-scale engagement of an organization such as learning maps, dialogue mats, trade fairs and large-scale events that are focused on building a common context for change/strategy. Second, tools that are focused on the delivery of tangible results including Work-Out, labs and incubation events.

Description of the tools and techniques

The group concluded that in addition to the three key areas of leadership, trust and training the other essential ingredient was an approach accompanied by a technique or toolset that could be applied at different times, used by various groups within the firm and/or used as a means to collaborate between firms. These tools offer the organization a mechanism to homogenize strategies across the organization and act as a binding agent when multiple strategies must be put into play simultaneously. Although each company employs these tools in different ways, the following is a synopsis of the most discussed tools and techniques where practitioners have annotated the process, use and expected results when using each tool.

Labs

Overview: Highly time-pressured and controlled environment for experimenting with new ways of working. Labs are a dedicated space with supporting techniques, tools and resources. This intervention is used to address intractable issues that are of critical importance to the business.

It creates action by breaking through the barriers that constrain the people or organization.

Process: a high level of coaching and facilitation taking the participants through an iterative cycle of ever-increasing breakthroughs and breakdowns. The work of the Lab is highly action-oriented and engages large areas of the business in new ways of working without putting any part of the business at risk. Resource and timing – six to ten people for the duration of the Lab. Scoping is up to four weeks, running of the Lab is typically a four to six-week time-boxed period.

When to use: Target key strategic issues and intractable business issues. Initial diagnostic of business situation challenges that traditional approaches have failed to address issues complicated by politics or turf.

Results: Produces breakthrough action on the business issue identified. Clarifies how results can be rapidly delivered and provides the forward actions. Labs generate accountability and ownership amongst the participants and those parts of the organization involved in the work. Generates leadership alignment around the solution and anticipated results. Creates a new way of working that is sustainable with the wider organization enrolled and supportive of changes.

Work-Out^{TM48}

Overview: A three-phased approach to engaging the front-line staff in taking accountability for operational improvements in under 90 days. This intervention is used to address operational and tactical issues. Best results are when there are 'scaleable' issues – that is a task/role/process repeated many times.

Process: Three phases: scoping, a three-day event and 90 days of implementation. The facilitated three-day meeting identifies the core problems, creates innovative solutions and presents these to a leadership panel for an immediate Yes/No decision. Resource and timing – scoping is typically two weeks. About 15–40 front-line staff attend the three-day event. The 90-day implementation is carried out in the line with minimal support.

When to use: Only on operation or tactical issues. Where there is a need to engage staff in the 'culture' of change – typically before a larger change programme is implemented. Any area of the business where there is a considerable amount of repeated work. Areas of the business that have been in existence for more than ten years – they have had time to calcify.

Results: Between 6 and 16 operational changes implemented producing benefits that are typically four times the cost of the event. All participants engage in supporting the implementation phase. Improved relationship between front-line staff (participants) and leadership (decision panel). All participants taking greater accountability for improving their own working environment. Generates other opportunities and ideas (parked because they were out of scope) that can be further progressed outside of Work-Out™ using more appropriate techniques.

Mass mobilization

Overview: Mass mobilization sessions take attendees through a self-diagnostic and some process of co-creation around a selected issue. This generates shared ownership of change with a large number of key people in the business. The exact time frame and number of people involved depends on the size of the organization, number of locations and geographic dispersion. The bringing together of over 75 members of staff (typically in excess of 100) to address certain aspects of change.

Process: A series of interviews to inform the design and then a large two to three-day meeting. Typical agenda follows a diagnostic and then topic focus (trade-fare) and then commitment to action (contracting process). Event typically captured on video to help with communication to a wider audience. Resource and timing – two to four weeks to design and typically two to three days and up to 150 attendees.

When to use: First, during the roll out of a business change when the organization moves from concept work to implementation. When a company introduces change using a process of small incremental releases it seeks to capture organizational learning and knowledge during the change effort, aiming to overcome the organization's national resistance to change. Second, when there is a need to shift how senior managers lead and engage the organization through a complex business change. When needing to enrol the 'bottleneck' (senior- and middle-level managers). Third, when all employees need to be engaged to achieve results. Fourth, when rapid enrolment is required.

Results: Clear participation of wider group in change process. Capture of front-line knowledge. Alignment of organization behind value/change. Early warning of employee issues. Significant grass roots change and action. Increased motivation and reduced cynicism.

Trade fair

Overview: As the idea sounds, it is a market for a set of refined concepts, displayed in a 'trade fair' environment of booths to solicit input and feedback from the participants. Senior executives circulate around the booths, learn concepts and then give feedback at the end of the session.

Process: Teams develop concepts over a two to five-day period based on a scope and charter established at the outset. They then detail the concepts, including supporting analysis (e.g. strategy, cost/benefit simulations), resource requirements and implementation plans. Each team builds a booth and market their ideas. Executives visit each booth, learning about the concepts. Executive team provides feedback and decisions at the end of the session to each team on how to move forward: Red/Amber/Green teams then organize into action for delivery. Resource and timing – up to two weeks planning in teams and half a day and up to 150 attendees.

When to use: When you need to engage the senior team in many issues that are at various stages of development. When you need to help the senior team develop ownership of the areas being developed. When you need to create a competitive nature amongst several teams. When you need to announce to the organization that new changes are going to happen.

Results: Rapid engagement of the leadership in new ideas and change. A market of ideas that leads to the ideas being delivered into action and owned by teams. Great for new strategy, product, concepts and market propositions.

Contracting process or valentines exercise

Overview: A facilitated conversation in the form of requests and commitments that drives targeted action and rapidly creates business results.

Process: Divide people into 'natural' working teams. Formulate 'Requests', ask for 'Clarification', and formalize 'Commitments' to deliver specific results. Requests include a selected committed partner (an individual from the other team that will make the promise), clearly state the issue and inhibitors and if necessary give suggested resolutions. Promises are signed by the selected committed partner, focused (not hold another meeting to decide what to do), must clearly state the required actions, results and associated parties and must specify the related dates. Resource and timing – three to six staff in each team working on an issue. Can be completed in a single day.

When to use: For clarifying key opportunities in the business, and for resolving unspoken blockages in the organization. Can be used as part of a large adaptive change programme, to identify the challenges and create a sense of urgency.

Results: Firm commitments to make improvements based on specific requests. Used successfully to rapidly simulate and agree prototype business offerings. Better for resolving short-term 'working' issues versus longer-term strategy.

Ringii

Overview: Ringii is a process of syndication that aligns a leadership team around a complex business topic without the need to gather the whole team together. This intervention is based on a technique that is well proven in Asian businesses where generating alignment without too much confrontation is critical. The key distinction here is to move from the 'Western' approach to facts, logic and selling to an 'Eastern' approach of opinions, synthesis and negotiation.

Process: A series of conversations seeking individual's opinions (not facts), uncovering conflicts, synthesizing a new overarching opinion (sometimes in the form of the value metric), negotiation and then formal agreement (alignment). This work is done through a 'Ringii Master' or team who are outside the leadership team and have no alliances. Resource and timing – a single 'Ringii Master' to complete the process. Typically a series of sessions over a month.

When to use: When leadership alignment is needed but time pressures, diaries and politics make it impossible to get everyone together. It can be also used when logic has failed to generate alignment or when the politics cannot be surfaced in public or when there is an unclear or emergent business issue around which leadership needs to be aligned.

Results: Leadership alignment around a key business issue. Clarity among the leadership team on how to judge the success of progress on this business issue.

Operating state diagnostic

Overview: A diagnostic for developing an understanding of major business issues, problems and areas of opportunity. Also enables the correct selection of the appropriate approach and tools to attack the issues.

Process: Several different approaches (interviews/meetings/questionnaire) that gather input from all the different functional areas and from different layers of the organization. At a simple level, this diagnostic can be run through a combination of focus groups, interviews and half-day workshops. At a more detailed level, a mini-lab can be used to create a menu of change opportunities. Resource and timing – a few weeks of interviews and one to two-day workshop with management team to confirm or refine the findings.

When to use: When the scope of change required is unclear or at the start of a change programme. When there are real or perceived barriers to change. To introduce a common vocabulary for change. To identify the behavioural shifts required implementing change.

Results: Programme for actions including the selection of the correct tools and techniques, as well as the appropriate participants for follow on work. Graphic representation of operating state. Alignment over barriers to change. Identified and prioritized behavioural shifts.

Value disciplines/metrics[49]

Overview: A diagnostic specifically focused on the strategy and operating model of a business. Derives a dominant metric (measure) for the business that enables action and decision making at all levels of the organization.

Process: Delivered via a combination of initial interviews followed up with a series of two to three-day workshops to generate alignment. If redefinition of the operating model is deemed necessary, this work usually follows on from the assessment with a lab. Resource and timing – typically completed in a few weeks with a series of interviews and workshops, effort is minimal.

When to use: Use when there is a need to clarify the future direction of the business, draw out sources of contention and misalignment. The current operating model is delivering diminishing returns. The organization is torn between too many or an ambiguous direction, and is failing at executing the strategy. Business environment is experiencing major change (e.g. Merger and acquisition activity, deregulation, consolidation and downsizing). Use when there is a lack of a consistent vocabulary for value or when source of competitive advantage is unclear or to replace unwanted measures of success.

Results: Agreement on sources of value and threshold value. Common vocabulary around sources of value. Energized change agenda. Clarity about what is not to be pursued beyond threshold levels. Precise and measurable definition of value. Team aligned on delivery of value. Input to reward and remuneration process.

Seven S diagnostic[50]

Overview: A diagnostic of the organization to focus on seven areas. *Strategy*: a set of actions that you start with and must maintain. *Structure*: how people and tasks are organized. *Systems*: all the processes and information flows that link the organizations together. *Style*: how managers behave. *Staff*: how you develop managers (current and future). *Superordinate goals*: longer-term vision, and all that values stuff, that shapes the destiny of the organization. *Skills*: dominant attributes or capabilities that exist in the organization.

Process: For each of the different 'S' categories, first identify the current state, then the desired state. Note which areas need to be changed, are good and bad. Determine the appropriate actions. Can also be used to help at an event by giving the different S's to different teams. Resource and timing – typically completed in a single day with anything from six to over one hundred attendees. It is important to have representatives from across the business. This process will take longer if interviews are used.

When to use: When a business-wide audit of key success drivers is required. When there is a lack of a coherent model for understanding the current business state. In an environment when alignment is achieved via a more analytical approach. When a team needs to take a wider perspective of the change remit. In the first week of a lab (see the section on labs).

Results: The Seven S assessment is a clear understanding of the critical strengths and weaknesses of the organization. A strong indication of the areas to focus on supporting or affecting if change is to stick.

Putting the tools to work collaboratively

Armed with an arsenal of techniques and methodologies for collaborations, Grunwald asks two fundamental questions: to what extent are strategies 'devised' and to the extent that anything is devised, can it be done 'collaboratively'? Grunwald presents an example to consider by examining the 1970s, when blue jeans became extremely fashionable worldwide. ICI, a British chemical company was a leading manufacturer in the fast-growing artificial fibres business. They were planning a major investment in a new terephthalic acid plant (TPA), being a precursor of terylene. The figures all added up, the trends were shooting in the right directions, the charts looked good, the returns were impressive and the Board approved the project, the biggest single investment in ICI's history at that time.

Unfortunately, blue jeans are made out of cotton, not terylene. The figures, which the investment was based, looked as shown in Figure 3.3. Unfortunately, the investment strategy was a disaster. In another part of the company, there was an old plant producing indigo dye. It had not made much money for years, and was on the point of being shut down. Nevertheless, the craze for blue jeans, demanding indigo, suddenly made it ICI's star performer. The company developed an indigo strategy.

At a broad level, this strategy was not devised; rather, it emerged. The devising came at a more detailed level, lower down. On the other hand, the collaboration came at a higher level, at the company's HQ and its

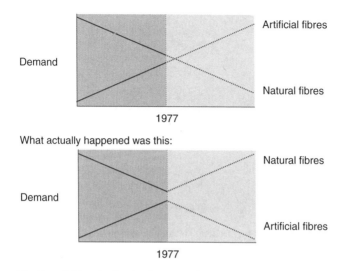

Figure 3.3 Use of fibres in Denim-Jeans production

Main Board. These people saw one strategy failing catastrophically while another succeeded unexpectedly, and adjusted their own overall strategy, accordingly. Such adjustment was not possible at the level of the TPA and indigo businesses; it needed a broader viewpoint.

The point that Grunwald brings to the forefront of our thinking is that the more a strategy needs to be 'devised' the more difficult it is to collaborate. The truly collaborative strategies are those that emerge through a combination of internal actions and external events.

The key to collaboration is communication

The value of complete strategic awareness according to Jones is to engage the total collective talent of a firm in the strategy-developing process by engaging a non-traditional process in which collaboration is a timed process. Detailed collaboration using traditional methods of strategy development is not viable when you have more than ten staff. However, there is real value in having everyone aware of the strategy as new ideas filter up from within.

The traditional method of strategy development is based on the premise that those at the top of the organization, or those close by, are where the relevant knowledge resides – the small number, typically less than ten would be involved in strategy development and this would involve each person being aligned $\Sigma n - 1$ $(n - 1)$ conversations/agreements as illustrated in Figure 3.4.

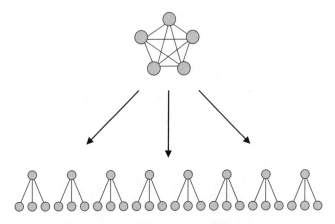

Figure 3.4   Traditional hierarchical strategy development

If every individual in the organizational hierarchy had to be consulted in order to collaborate on the development of the strategy, the resulting time required to collect, collate and assimilate everyone's point of view would then paralyse the organization. This traditional top-down approach is predicated on the concept that top management and/or specialized strategist are in communication with key customers and have the capability to look across the marketplace to devise strategies that closely align to the financial commitments of the firm and stockholders. One could argue that this command-and-control method of strategy development works well when the brains of the organization are at the top and everyone else is a simply under-educated worker incapable of independent thought. This ideal may have been true in distant previous generations in the history of automating the factory floor but it does not represent the workforce of modern business. The top-down method is founded on the use of analysis by senior managers to develop strategic initiatives. As Mintzberg points out this approach has one glaring flaw: 'because analysis is not synthesis, strategic planning is not strategy formation'.[51] In Mintzberg's view, analysis by individuals that are removed from the business process can precede or follow strategy development but it is not a substitute for union of thoughts and ideas that come from the wisdom and knowledge of front-line managers. Strategies which originate from centralized strategy organization often act to wipe out or retard the value generating capabilities of front line business units as observed by Goold, Campbell and Alexander in their groundbreaking research on multibusiness corporations: 'The conclusion

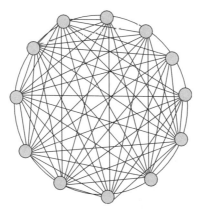

Figure 3.5   Involving every operating group in strategy development

we reach is that, while a few successful parents create value in multi-business companies, the large majority are value destroyers.'[52]

The other extreme, which Bradley points out – which clearly is not viable for large organizations, is total involvement in strategy development by every operating group in the firm as illustrated in Figure 3.5. This methodology works when organizations are small, such as in a software development company of less than 100 people, because groups are small enough and conversations can be rapidly facilitated. In the case of small organizations, the intimate knowledge of the operations is often a result of having to do multiple jobs or a continual redefinition of job functions during the growth of the firm. Additionally, the personal relationships developed with a smaller firm makes decision making more intimate in that there are few layers between decision makers and the day-to-day activities.

However, Bradley suggests a hybrid approach whereby the corporation establishes a mechanism to ensure first that business units are made aware of early strategic thoughts, and second that they should provide a means for new thoughts and ideas originating within the business units to push up through the organization's hierarchy to inform the strategic thinking process, as reflected in Figure 3.6. This approach is valuable because it is built on a concept that individuals at the front line of the business have a stake in the products, services and relationships with clients while fulfilling the goal of senior management to transform strategic planning into a 'living' or self-regenerating process.[53] In this model, the pre-communication of new ideas and early strategic thoughts

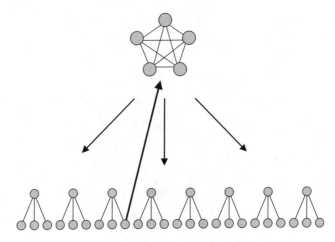

Figure 3.6　Hybrid approach to strategy development

to front-line personnel in turn stimulates the next generation of new ideas and creates involvement across the firm. The key is to educate individuals to the timeliness and depth of their contribution. In all cases, once ideas are submitted to the process of strategy development, feedback to the individual is paramount to the future generation of strategy. Individuals have an inherent curiosity to know what happened to their contribution: is the firm acting on it or not and if not why.

One thing that corporations often overlook is that the synthesis of ideas is more important than the generation of ideas, as Koch notes:

> Originality in strategic thinking is of much less importance than synthesising what is already available, being clear about where it is most useful and about the trade-offs between different approaches, and putting the heart of strategy back where it belongs, in the messy entrails of business unit reality.[54]

Developing the strategic corporate competency

During the book-writing event, Abuel-Ealeh asked two key questions: how does an organization take a geographically dispersed set of capable individuals and create a collaborating strategic competency? Can there ever be true 'collaboration', even on an internal level, in strategy development?

What does it mean, first, to devise strategy collaboratively? According to Abuel-Ealeh, collaboration would imply that there would be equity of the parties in the development of strategy. Essentially, collaborators would be an extension, albeit on a great scale, of the strategic development team acting less like planners and more like synthesizers. Collaborators do more than simply insert new ideas as input to a process of strategy development. They employ analytical and methodological skills to elaborate on their contribution in a dialogue with others ultimately refining and honing their ideas. To achieve this, in many organizations a philosophical adjustment in the command-and-control structure of strategy development must occur whereby the traditional managers of strategy become facilitators of the strategy process and not the approval authority of ideas and suggestions.

Practically, how could this be done? Abuel-Ealeh believes that departments or teams within an organization are a vital source of input into the strategic planning process and their input must be facilitated in different ways, taking into account the most appropriate method for the audience – usually experimental. Regardless of the mechanisms for getting this input, and the style in which it is devised, the most productive result will be a set of relatively disparate strategic aims, which must be put together in order to gain a cohesive whole. Potentially, the least productive result would be a set of action points from each department (though not necessarily department focused, which would be positive!), which do not give enough direction to form a coherent strategy. Abuel-Ealeh notes that there will always be a need for leadership in the development of strategy – after all, how would the workforce input into a process if no one instigates it in the first place? To some extent, there is flexibility in how the process is led or orchestrated.

First, the composition of the leadership needs to be dynamic. There is no reason why the team that directs the process and creates the cohesive whole cannot be an entirely new team. If there exists already a commitment to the value of the opinion of the whole organization, then surely it would be a natural step to create a team from across all sectors of the organization to coordinate the process. The leaders of the organization may well be more experienced, more adept at pulling together the sum of the parts, but, in practice, it would send a more accessible message to the rest of the organization that the process into which they have inputted will be coordinated by their peers.

Second, the style of the leadership must change as the business conditions warrant. Even if the coordinating team is comprised of the organizational leaders, it is key to know which leadership style is appropriate use – when is it time to be a dictator, when do you need to facilitate? Equally important, this must be made clear at the start of the collaborative process.

In Abuel-Ealeh's view, an organization can fail if the style of leadership is wrong for a particular part of the planning process. For example, an authoritative style may be more suitable for an organization that has never been involved in a similar exercise, but in order to synthesize the best from the team during the strategic planning process the leadership style will also have to be facilitative. To gain the most from the action planning stage, it could well be seen that the ideal style is delegate – departments or internal teams are better placed to develop action plans than leaders are. However, someone still needs to champion the process; otherwise, the action stage will never come to fruition. Therefore, there is still a reason for the authoritarian style to come into play. Thus, collaboration still needs to be driven by strong leadership, and with an insight into what leadership style suits the occasion or the organization best.

Innovation as part of collaborative strategy

Southward reminds us that in tough markets, where cost cutting as a means of growing profitability is nearing an end, innovation becomes an even more important capability for organizations as a means of driving the marketplace and securing its competitive position. Corporations strive to increase revenues from their established marketplaces in one of two ways: by an increase in the size of the market, or by improving their competitive position within the market. Innovation, in Southward's perspective, is a way of achieving both methods of revenue enhancement while becoming a critical capability in it own right. Innovation must be a key part of the business leader's decision-making process in determining the best organizational structure for collaborative strategy.

Traditionally, people have viewed innovation in terms of breakthrough discoveries and fortunate accidents, rather than as the result of a focused effort and good business planning. As Southward points out, successful innovation is not an event. Innovation must be a part of everyday business operation and every employee should be tasked to think of how to make improvements whether on the job or within a marketplace. In addition, market-changing innovation requires a focus and dedication of key employees and they should be allowed the time and resources to innovate in many different ways. Innovation is not random, and can emerge whenever there is a structure to inspire it.

Innovating effectively requires concentrating on gaining the right structure, focusing on interdependencies, targeting the right capabilities and making it happen. Companies that follow this course make innovation a sustained and perpetual part of their management and operational disciplines. There is mounting evidence that regardless of organization's structure unless the procedures using traditional criteria to evaluate innovation projects are revamped the formal structure often stifles innovation.[55] Diana Thomas, from the Institute of Leadership and Management, asks the fundamental question of whether innovation is the outcome of an imaginative response to a future possibility or a process, which in many corporations is simply not future-orientated but simply past-derived. Therefore, process improvements are essentially a response to a long-standing 'grouse'; as past-derived and therefore maybe moving on a slower cycle of information/reaction. With innovations, either you 'catch the moment' or you have missed it. In the case of process improvements, the grouse is not going to go away; therefore, it may not be so time-critical to capture the response as it occurs.

Capabilities and structure

Getting the right structure involves looking at the business as a portfolio of capabilities rather than as organizational silos. A capability such as product development, customer relationship management describes how a company comes together in terms of its people, processes and technology. A key focus should be in building the right organizational structures to collaborate and harness 'collective intelligence'.

A company generates revenue by using its capabilities and leveraging the knowledge and experience of its employees. The company's earning capacity and profit potential is therefore limited by the sum of its capabilities. When developing organizational structures, this has to be borne in mind. People, politics, ineffective processes and communication issues all serve to reduce the organization's effectiveness and thereby deliver an overall capability that is less than the sum of its individual parts. This can limit an organization's ability to make profit. Using the firm's capabilities to formulate and execute collaborative strategies requires a focus on how work is done rather than on how the company is structured. In many cases, the firm must adapt its current structure to align more closely with the business needs to be collaborative allowing for the establishment of a collective intelligence and higher rate of communication throughout the organization.

An overall capability view is critical for innovation, as it enables executives to think of the components of the business in terms that they can manage both individually and as a portfolio. Capabilities extend beyond corporate structures and often involve the abilities of customers, suppliers and other third parties. Technology and the Internet in particular have dramatically reduced the cost of collaboration, making capability sourcing particularly important to innovation and competitive advantage.

Targeting innovation efforts

For strategic thinking, it is useful to appreciate that not all business capabilities are equal. Some are needed to support the ongoing business but do not serve to deliver competitive advantage. Others do serve to provide differentiation and these need to be protected and developed as they can often be easily copied.

Targeting innovation efforts involves understanding the relative contribution of each capability that can be broadly categorized into types of capabilities:

- Differentiating capabilities, which help it to achieve profitability by providing the organization with a source of competitive advantage. These capabilities help the company to distinguish itself in the marketplace.
- Core capabilities, which are critical to the business, but they do not necessarily differentiate the company. Poor performance of core capabilities often compromises a company's cost structure and customer service performance.
- Supporting capabilities that are still important to the business but only exist in order to allow the company the means to deliver its core and differentiated capabilities. These can be regarded as a 'hygiene factor'.

Those capabilities that are a source of differentiation and competitive advantage are normally those that the company will want to in-source and develop its innovation and expertise to further drive changes in the market and protect an organization's competitive position. Close consideration should be given to outsourcing those capabilities that do not provide a source of competitive advantage.

Making innovation happen

Every organization must think about how to improve its operations and better serve its customers. Taking action to make innovation happen involves more than brainstorming sessions. It requires three fundamental actions:

- *Innovating through simulating.* Use business simulation to 'test' innovative ideas and replace executive indecision with knowledge and confidence.
- *Managing with measures.* Measures and innovation are not contradictory. Performance measures provide the information necessary to manage the benefits of innovation rather than relying on luck.

- *Making innovation part of the core.* Innovative thinking must become part of the skill set of executives, managers and line personnel. Innovation is too important to leave to chance. Companies must continually extend their capabilities to maintain hard-won customers and generate profitable growth, even during difficult times. That requires making successful innovation a continuous part of the organization's every day activities, innovation itself should become a core of differentiated capabilities.

Dealing with ambiguity and unpredictable events

> *Axiom: Within business process ambiguity and market uncertainty lay the rudiments of opportunity.*

Even under the best corporate efforts to predicting the future, factors such as market demand, customer behaviours, political stability and many other components of modern capitalism at times render the best strategic plans valueless or cause strategies to denigrate into reactionary tactical manoeuvres. One of the key factors that alter strategic intent is the organization's ability to handle and manage both the ambiguities of the business environment, and the uncertainties that permeate from within the organization. Corporations that appear to be market leaders are still limited in their ability to predict market trends and customer behaviour because of ambiguous information from the markets they serve. In the case of well-run companies, this inability to predict does not necessarily indicate the absence of strategic planning rigour. The depth and rigour of their strategy development methodologies act to offset the limitations in resolving complex market phenomenon. The US Geological survey has recognized that as the disciplinary breadth of an organization's interdisciplinary efforts increases, so too must the understanding of the inherent limits in predictability including the social sciences and their methodologies dealing explicitly with ambiguity is an important feature of interdisciplinary science.[56]

With the purpose of exploring how organizations cope with the topic of ambiguity, one can argue that an organization's ability to handle market ambiguity and unpredictable events is directly proportional to four aspects of corporate behaviour, namely, an understanding of the factors that influence the markets in which it operates, the development of a process to guide reactions to changing conditions, discipline within the firm to think strategically to avoid the temptation to only act tactically, and more importantly, rethink its value added to the marketplace. Therefore the key to dealing with the unknown or the unpredictability of the global business environment is, in Quinn's words,

> The very essence of strategy – whether military, diplomatic, business, sports, (or) political [...] – is to *build a posture* that is so strong (and potentially flexible) in selective ways that the organization can achieve its goals despite the unforeseeable ways external forces may actually interact when the time comes.[57]

Events such as the September 11 terrorist attacks are indeed unpredictable; however, that they are going to occur is not. Therefore, understanding the relativity of these events to the firm's ability to deliver value and the impact of catastrophic events on demand is not a matter of reactive surprise, but an issue in the depth of planning. To understand the relative nature of proactive and reactive strategic thinking, we offer a framework in which to categorize the relationships between market demand and long-term corporate objectives as illustrated in Figure 3.7.

It is naive to think that within a large organization, a 'one strategy fits all' philosophy can be developed and sustained. As organizations grow

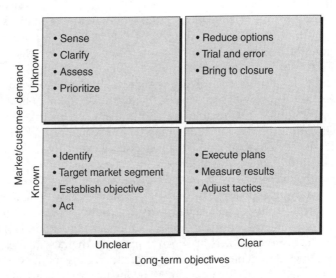

Figure 3.7 Ambiguity and objectives

and adapt to new market conditions, they will inherently develop strategies that address topics such as markets, products, customers and suppliers or they will devise strategic initiatives to focus resources on strategic objectives such as eCommerce, new market entry, a new technology or a specialized market segment. Therefore, within a firm, multiple types of strategies and various approaches to strategy formulation coexist which act to diversify the organization's ability to anticipate unknown events. Corporations can find themselves in the envious position of executing multiple overlapping strategies due to a comprehensive multi-organizational coordinated strategy process, or the unenviable position of multiple strategies resulting from a lack of communication between operating strategy development groups in which multiple strategies are competing for resources within the firm. The latter often represents the bulk of today's corporations in which the autonomy of business units allows them to create strategies that do not span hierarchical organizational lines.

In Shirreff's view, organizations must establish a clear approach to set and fine-tune their strategic intentions in ways that make each approach to strategy flexible, first, to meet new conditions, and second, to adapt to totally unexpected events. As new business conditions occur, strategies that previously seemed perfectly clear and unambiguous will require period reinterpretation to remain viable. As new conditions stretch the credibility of the strategy, as it was formerly understood, the strategy must also be adapted to them. To Shirreff, corporate strategies are vulnerable to low-frequency, high-impact events in two ways; events which are thinkable (such as terrorist attack, fire, earth quake) and ones that have not yet been thought of such as a new technological invention originating in a far-off market suddenly making your product worthless. Shirreff points out that it is likely that there should be a limit, however, to the level of worst-case scenario that a company could meaningfully survive. For example, the onset of a nuclear winter might eliminate the entire market of a tourism company or wider market. In this case, there is not much point in having a strategy for such a disaster, except perhaps for minimizing loss of life.

However, Shirreff makes an important distinction; there are indeed thinkable, foreseeable freakish events and changes of circumstances that would be survivable and would be worth planning. It is valuable to rehearse the response to such catastrophic events even if the scenario rehearsed is only one of many that are possible. Shirreff's line of thinking is reflected in the *year 2025* US Air Force study, which realizes that the key to strategy lies in the organization's ability to close the gap between the event and the response to any future scenario:

> Superiority may derive as much from improved thinking about the employment of current capabilities and the rapid integration of existing technologies as from the development of technological breakthroughs.[58]

However, in the corporate world, the ability to develop probable future scenarios is limited to the finite amount of investment in the strategy process, thereby reducing the number of pre-planned possibilities and responses. The strategy process should make a company more flexible in its approach to business because it presents more options and a wider range of alternative solutions. Strategies must anticipate the future by identifying trends and future scenarios, formulating a core and contingent response, accumulating resources to implement the response and, finally, operating by executing the core strategy, thus monitoring the environment and execute or abandon options as circumstances dictate.[59] The key point that Shirreff makes is that strategies are predictions of the future, that is, they act as a mechanism to project what could be achieved by the organization under a specific set of conditions. So as to leverage the resources of the firm, Shirreff advocates that role-playing games and brainstorming sessions can be very useful, especially if they involve those at many levels of the firm with direct experience of systems and processes that might be affected. This is another argument for involving individuals at all levels in scenario planning and strategic thinking to instil an awareness of disaster recovery procedures and a consciousness of what are strategically the most vital components of the business.

One could argue that dealing with ambiguity at all levels is more than a process of understanding future states and mitigating risks; rather, it is also a skill that can be learned, mentored and measured. Increasingly, we find evidence of this as dealing with ambiguity, according to the Meta Group, is one of the four key measurements for Chief Information Officers (CIO). Due to the nature of the technology industry, a CIO must be comfortable with continual change, variations because of new technologies, the transformational impact of a technological implementation and in dealing with risks associated with implementations. CIOs invariably cope with high degrees of uncertainty, when technologies are applied to the operations of the firm, the business processes and the varying levels of communications required to sustain the momentum while a project is underway. As a leader of change, a CIO must be able to rapidly adjust to new conditions, view strategic initiatives from multiple perspectives, build multi-organizational teams and work across many operating environments. As the Meta Group claims, the key skill for a CIO is a strong pattern of recognition skills in data, information and business, permitting him or her to act and decide without requiring the total picture, confirming patterns and proactively teaching their organizations about the updated information and knowledge models.[60]

Another perspective on the dealing with ambiguity is Perez-Novoa's view on the importance of corporations in the private and public sectors to incorporate an unpredictability factor into their planning process so that over time they learn how to deal with unpredictable events. In economic terms, corporations should add the term 'aleatory variable', meaning that strategies must include planned uncertainty into their business model.[61] Although planned uncertainty sounds like an oxymoron, there is uncertainty in every plan, and although a solution for a given set of conditions is not always predictable, a placeholder in the plan with an associated process for resolution must be considered. In simple terms, unpredictable events eventually occur regardless of how well a plan is crafted; the value is not in second-guessing the solution, but in having a process that when required rapidly facilitates the solution. In this case, strategists and leaders need to sense the market constantly and be aware of the global economy context since unpredictable events come mainly from industry, legal or macroeconomic environments rather than internal issues which can be managed within the organization's boundaries.

Perez-Novoa considers the case of unpredictability in capital markets which are subject to an enormous array of unpredictable events, mostly coming from microeconomic issues. For example, a mining analyst needs to manage a downturn in price of gold or copper. The analyst has to predict a contingency plan if the market of gold falls down or otherwise he will lose a huge amount of other's money. The strategy in this case has to come from the bottom or the 'analyst'. He or she has the responsibility of making the investments attractive. Although the bank would support the analyst if something occurs, he or she would be responsible for a tragedy. Risk management is extremely important. From Perez-Novoa's perspective, strategists are not only the managers, but so also is everyone in the firm that deals with economic and financial performance of a company. Every analyst is a strategist in the capital markets area, since their investment recommendations are the basis for investors in order to inject money in the financial system.

Looking at ambiguity in a different light, Leaton-Gray provides us with a view where every business contains some unpredictable factors that affect its performance, its ability to serve customers and to motivate employees, variations that are often difficult to capture and articulate within a strategy. This is inevitable and is normally dealt with by defining the strategy in such a way that the resulting variations can be coped with by adopting a series of tactics rather than tearing up the strategic plan and starting again. However, according to Leaton-Gray, there will also be occasions where you genuinely cannot attempt to define the likely outcomes because of a significant ambiguity in the future. An obvious example of this is in an industry's relationship with the government. If your industry is about to have a major change in the nature or extent of regulation, it may be unclear what kind of environment will exist in just a few years' time. You can just throw your hands in the air and say, 'who knows what'll happen. Let's just leave things as they are, and hope that it all comes alright in the end'. Leaton-Gray calls this the '*que sera sera*' approach, one which assumes that your contacts in government, or your lobbyist, are so good that you will get the outcome you need. Caricaturizing, Leaton-Grey exemplifies another approach: 'I had a quiet word with the Minister over dinner and he assured me, we'll be alright.' This is the 'a word in his ear' approach.

Unfortunately, the increased levels of global competition demands that corporations plan for and address ambiguity by assessing a range of possible financial performance and other measurable outcomes. Organizations developing strategies must now ask themselves how various types of unpredictable events such as terrorism, catastrophic loss, brand disasters like tainted products and other unanticipated events affect the company and its strategy. Regardless of the type of unplanned event, are the outcomes ultimately very different from each other?

In Leaton-Gray's view, all too often there is an assumption that the changes from an unpredictable event are themselves unpredictable. Frequently this is not the case. Our knowledge of the sector, the legislators, the competitors and our company will often give us a quite limited range of likely results. When the Communications bill was being discussed in the United Kingdom and regulation of the media and telecommunications was about to be brought under one super-regulator it was always going to be unlikely that a complete amalgamation of the previous regulatory regimes was going to occur. Content regulation on the telephones would not have been popular, with British Telecom told not to allow its customers to discuss sex on their phones before the nine o'clock watershed. Financial regulation of the media has now evolved, with ITV being able to broadcast anything it liked, as long as it charged its customers according to a set tariff. Therefore, although any regulatory regime could theoretically occur the range of truly likely outcomes could be narrowed down substantially and the strategic reaction to each scenario planned.

Building on this idea, that there is some degree of predictability in unpredictable events, Roe points out that some risks are at least known, if not predictable, such as currency fluctuations or oil price fluctuations, and business has become very adept at managing these risks through mechanisms such as hedging. However, there are always risks that are unknown or unquantifiable; the key to surviving these is keeping a sufficient number of somewhat diverse options open for as long as possible. Roe makes a significant point in describing this process: 'In other words, operating a number of different business lines whilst simultaneously keeping options open and making decisions when you have to, and not before.' It is important to note that this does not mean delaying decision making beyond the optimum time as this just adds to the uncertainty of the business.

Roe relates the case of a now defunked strategy consulting company employing around 1000 people worldwide. In 1998, the management began offering its customers a competency in Internet strategy development, for example, they were involved in Egg.com and a number of other early Internet business. At the height of the dot-com boom, this rapidly became an attractive part of the business, providing the opportunity for cutting-edge thinking as well as lucrative fees. In 1999, the management decided to focus its entire business on the Internet and agreed a merger with a company providing Internet IT development, marketing and branding expertise. The merger added a strategy capability to the offering with obvious synergies. In 2000, the new company merged with an IT business delivering ERP/back office IT solutions, creating a one-stop-shop for customers' IT needs with obvious opportunities for cross-selling the various services. In April 2001, the newly merged strategy-Internet-technology company went bankrupt. In less than 18 months, the firm had gone from a profitable and growing strategy-consulting firm to bankruptcy. They did what proverbially is said as 'putting all one's eggs in one basket', and committed much earlier than necessary to the market evolution of eCommerce.

In Roe's view, there is a very powerful temptation for corporate leadership to follow a popular trend. Strategically, this may or may not be the right thing to do, if the goal of the business is to remain viable long term. Management teams must enable processes that act to build strategies from diverse perspectives within the organization to safeguard the firm's ability to cope with failure in any specific line of business.

One would expect leadership to be less risk adverse with shareholders' money than with their own. In the case of the strategy consulting firm, as partners they were also the shareholders and yet they were still willing to gamble millions of pounds of their own money on the Internet boom. They fell into the trap of believing their own analysis and forecasts that they only had been selling to clients. They believed, as did many in the technology industry, in their own propaganda.

Parker provides us with a historically based perspective on ambiguity and strategy development by reminding us that in some cases the underlying definition of strategy very often comes with implications of a final target. Churchill's strategy during 1940–45 was to 'win the war'. In this particular example, this strategy was sufficient. However, in 2003, the President Bush strategy of 'win the war' in Iraq was clearly inadequate and left a lot of untidy, though possibly not completely unpredictable, issues to be resolved. In Parker's view, strategy is not always a simple overarching structure that has a definite end, strategy must be defined in two ways: strategy is a high-level route map to a stated objective; or strategy is the setting of a direction for an organization.

As a roadmap to a stated objective, the results of a strategy's deployment can be measured easily. Parker relates the strategy from his own experience at EPCoT, whose strategic objectives are to deliver products and services that will be in a place to support new EU legislation coming into law in 2004. In this approach, the key is to set the objectives and measure the influence of events relative to the end goals.

Alternatively, Parker describes simple direction setting as an equally valid strategy, as found in UK government agencies when it becomes clear that there was no measurable or target endpoint, just a general direction that would change as the strategy is developed. This method, which requires a great deal of skill in dealing with ambiguity, is described by Parker in the following way: 'In defining the strategy, I used the analogy, we are heading towards France. We might think our destination is Paris, but we may find that we arrive in Lyon.'

Each type of strategy has its own certainties, uncertainties, risks and ambiguities. What was unpredicted in the 'win the war in Iraq' strategy was looting and general public disorder, which was not a problem in the Churchill strategy. Generally, the definition of strategy has unpredictability constraining the end goal rather than built into its process of development. Organizations that adopt the direction setting approach to strategy development have unpredictability and ambiguity as built-in factors that must be managed proactively. Parker cautions that this approach requires a rigorous approach to resource management because the project manager will tend to say, build in slack and flexibility and the unpredictability can be managed.

Clearly, it is important to predict as many risks as possible and to plan for their successful mitigation using mechanisms such as the standard likelihood/impact/control matrix to define which are needed to reduce specific risks. Nevertheless, there will always be unpredictable events that need accommodating. Parker relates the story of Lloyds of London in the early 1990s having built their market based on being able to deal with two major world catastrophes. When Lloyds were hit by the possible, but low probability of three major world catastrophes – the environmental pollution by the sinking of oil tankers, the litigation around asbestos and the severe damage caused by extreme weather conditions – the events led Lloyds to review the mindset structure and workings and set up a new company (Equitas) to underwrite the whole market.

Lloyds had a personal strategy 'to build a house of substance appropriate to the plot'. Whilst having worked with the planners to design a house appropriate to the area, we did not predict that the house would be accepted by planners, turned down by councillors and the decision reinforced by an inspector who stated that our London suburb neighbours should have a right to a view of their own garden and the sky. Therefore, new plans that took the slope of the land into account were devised to lower the house by excavating foundations and altering roof construction. Even strategies with clear and simple aims can have unpredictable events that need to be dealt with as they arise. Parker's point is not to expect to be able to predict all future events (though do try to predict the obvious ones). When the unpredictable happens, regroup, learn, replan and make dealing with unpredictable events a process in its own right.

Risk analysis

One of the primary considerations within all strategy development is the analysis of risk. Organizations find it useful to categorize risk, because categorization leads to the formulation of assumptions on how to deal with or mitigate risks. Risks arise from a number of categories and their origins provide some insight on how risks can be managed and mitigated. In Parker's view, a good first division of risk is whether it is internal or external. Clearly, an external risk is one over which there is no possibility of reducing the risk, whereas an internal risk may have methods that will reduce its likelihood of occurring. Examples of external risks are the effect of interest rates, or the improvement of the delivery of a competitor. Internal risks could be control of cash flow, or the work delivered by research and development. Another categorization considers whether a risk falls into one of the following areas of the business: financial, strategic, operational or hazardous. An example of these types of risks is an external hazard – the effects of weather or an internal operational risk – the accounting controls.

Having identified the classes to which risk are to be allocated, the next question that Parker poses is how do you assess risks? Organizations can employ a variety of tools such as brainstorming, type analysis, checklists, process mapping, SWOT analysis (Strengths, Weaknesses, Opportunities and Threats), PEST analysis (Political, Economic, Social and Technical), and expert guidance. Once you have defined the categories of risks, and have spent time in defining the risks to your business, the next step is to rate the likelihood of impact on the company.

Figure 3.8 shows one approach to handling risk by defining the risk, assessing the likelihood of the risk occurring on a scale of 0 to 9 (0 means it will never occur, 9 means it is likely to occur frequently) and then assessing the impact of the risk using a similar scale. To establish the relative importance of each risk multiply these two numbers together to produce the effect that this will have on the organization. The risks with the highest numbers are the ones that should be addressed first.

However, in Parker's view what can be done to reduce risks is another question: If the effect is low, is it worth the cost of eliminating a risk? If the risk is purely external, eliminating a risk is not likely to be a possibility. Nevertheless, if the risk can be eliminated and the costs of doing so are reasonable, then this may be the approach to take. The organization may realize that some risks cannot be eliminated but can be controlled. The cabling example in Figure 3.8 should be able to be eliminated. However, there may be circumstances where temporary cables have to be used, so rules for controlling the environment around temporary cable use helps to control the risk. Sometimes, it is impossible to either control or eliminate risks. It is therefore important to have a plan to mitigate the risk. This is often just an insurance policy. However, a formal process that

Risk	Likelihood	Impact	Effect	Eliminate	Control	Mitigate
Death by Act of God	1	9	9	No	No	Yes
Accident falling over cables	5	7	35	Yes	Yes	No
Rain damage	4	2	8	No	No	Yes
Data corruption	3	9	27	No	Yes	Yes

Figure 3.8 Elements of risk

addresses risks may simply identify the circumstances around the risk making it more visible when the risk is likely to occur.

Morgan contends that once the strategy is developed, tactics agreed and work is preceding, risks are noted and actions are in place to manage them, to mitigate or avoid them if they turn up. This raises an important question: So what is going to go wrong now? In Morgan's view, there are two sources of pain that cannot be anticipated – ambiguity and unexpected events. Both require steady nerves to meet and resolve, since they will throw the organization off course if individuals abandon their strategy and focus exclusively on tactical issue or make decisions out of competitive panic.

Ambiguity in implementation is something that leaders need to understand in-depth and not avoid. In most cases, ambiguity is a consequence of delaying decisions until the latest point by which they must be made and in that way you keep your options open for as long as possible, retaining flexibility. The problem then is that the ambiguity makes people uncomfortable and the pressure to decide will mount the longer you keep options open. People within the organization often interpret this behaviour as being indecisive. Morgan offers a word of caution in that this method has one major drawback; the perceived indecisiveness is a disadvantage for morale and team momentum. This disadvantage can be reduced by communicating intentions often to all parties that have a stake in the decision. Information makes ambiguity more palatable.

Some ambiguities originate outside or as a consequence of the decision-making process which can kill a strategy. These ambiguities can arise from a variety of sources but one of which forms around governance, centering on who really owns the strategy and who is responsible for it. This struggle for power or control manifests itself in delays in the process of making important decisions, in arguments about budgets and in making key people (or other resources) available to implement the strategy. Any of these will delay progress for undetermined periods and, unless the causes are removed, they will continue to delay progress and may eventually make the strategy irrelevant or unachievable. Moreover, the most dangerous case occurs when the true cause is not a desire on someone's part to sabotage the strategy, but a desire on two competing executives to own it. In the first case, it is reasonably straightforward to see and then confront at the executive board; in the second case, however, it can be impossible to resolve. Unexpected events are the ones that you never believed would happen, or never even considered. They will not be in the list of risks; they may not even be a part of the collective experience of the organization. Therefore, when they happen the chances are that no one has an immediate remedy and indeed no remedy may be available, so recovery may have to be by improvisation.

Morgan offers an example that should be considered – which, in his words, since it is written down, is of course no longer unexpected! Organizations that provide data centre services, typically in support of outsourcing contracts, will manage the risks to service continuity. This will extend to placing a backup data centre, fully mirrored with an uninterruptible power supply, connected by wide bandwidth fibre optics, at a distance from the main centre that is greater than the radius of a nuclear explosion. Suppose now that one of these is sited near Derby (in England) and the other to the east of Nottingham. This area is not prone to damage from the sea or from earthquakes and the risk of these events might not be addressed. Therefore, if there were an earthquake that damaged the main data centre severely and cut the cables linking it to the backup centre, the resulting interruption to service might have severe effects and be difficult to recover.

Case study: TV Programme '24'   If you watched the TV Programme '24' (second series) you may have seen this example. In this part of the plot, terrorists have planted a nuclear bomb in the United States, in Los Angeles. Due to hard work and some luck, the bomb was discovered in time for it to be moved to the desert before it exploded, so causing little loss of life. Nonetheless, the United States has been attacked and evidence is produced that three countries in the Middle East conspired with the terrorists to carry this out. The president is placed with the decision to go to war on the strength of this evidence, analysis of which convinces almost everyone of its veracity; the few people who are not convinced believe that despite the seeming credibility that the evidence has been planted to start a war. They convince the president, who has already set the attack in motion, to stay the final decision until the last possible minute, to give them time to check the facts beyond any reasonable doubt. The resolution is unimportant; what is interesting is the amount of pressure the president is put under to make the decision and 'not tie the hands of the Joint Chiefs of Staff'. From their point of view, this delay severely increases the difficulty and risk of the operation. From another direction, the president's chief of staff notes that, not making the decision and not appearing on television to explain the situation, the president appears weak and indecisive and in consequence causes more public unrest. In the series, we believe the president is right to delay. In reality, and despite the real fear one would have of the consequence of such a war, would we be able to resist this pressure when there was rioting in the streets in part because nothing seemed to be being done? Here Morgan reiterates the perceptions generated by delaying decisions to keep flexibility, not allowing events to take control, not committing a resource prematurely when it may be needed elsewhere.

Inherent ambiguity

According to Morgan, when the surrounding situation in which the strategy is implemented remains ambiguous the problem is caused by unclear responsibilities.

Case study: ownership   Morgan describes a programme of business change that was being carried out to modernize the IT systems of a UK company that had recently been privatized. The work started but there were delays in making essential appointments such as the program director (implementation leader). There were also delays in clarifying the role and authority of the central team charged with supporting the work. The root cause of this lay with discussions at board level over who should own this – should it be the CIO as it was primarily an IT-led programme? Alternatively, should it be the Human Resources executive because of the impact on staff at a sensitive time, when there was already a lot of uncertainty and risk that key staff would leave or that the Trades Unions would lose confidence in the executive? Eventually, a director was appointed. However, the matter of ownership was never properly resolved, and the strategy was abandoned nine months later.

Case study: the delineation between IT and business   Morgan provides another case in which strategy implementation was undertaken by the IT department of an organization. The department undertook to supply hardware and software applications and to work with the organization to make sure that business processes and the hardware/software services converged to a point where they supported the expected results. However, the matter of ownership within the organization was not fully resolved, especially where changes to staff organization and roles were required. The CEO stated that such matters were outside the competency of IT and had to be resolved by the business. As issues arose, the resulting decision delays affected the department's work. IT then made some assumptions in order to make progress; assumptions that turned out to be unwarranted. Eventually the consequence of these assumptions affected the results sufficiently to affect the strategy. The strategy had to be abandoned, the CEO and CIO left the company, which was later sold on to another owner. The strategy, meant to bring them up to the competition, failed utterly.

Unexpected events

As a practising strategist on large projects, Morgan explains that unexpected events arise from left field, completely unforeseen, and unless you accept the minimal necessary damage to recover, you can make the situation worse and compromise the strategy completely. However, they also may be an opportunity to do things more effectively.

Case study: Air Traffic Control (ATC)   In the early 1990s, an ATC authority was developing a strategy that included significant cooperative work with the European ATC and with other countries. The outlines were in place and an important part of the work going forward was to upgrade the current IT systems, which were coming to the end of their useful life, while the details of a collaborative strategy were worked out. The upgrade did not involve replacement of hardware. Part of that work was to replace the 'message switch', the software that directs information about aircraft movements to the controller assigned to that aircraft. This is an important component of the system as it supports the correct and consistent division of airspace control at the landing approach. Unfortunately, the project to complete the upgrade was delayed by almost two years, due to two main causes. One, a change in requirements, could (and should!) have been foreseen and was eventually managed; the other cause was not predicted. At an early point in the project's life, there was a breakdown in the systems at a major airport which led to delays in landing. This had nothing to do with the project or with the message switch but one of the affected passengers happened to be a minister in the government at the time. A directive then was sent from the ministry of transportation to the effect that such delays should never happen again. The resulting change in underlying technology to 24 hours a day – 7 days a week, working altered the hardware on which the message switch was being developed. The impact was not fully considered and as a result, the project was not correctly restarted – corners were cut and this eventually delayed progress even further. This project delay meant that another interim strategy had to be worked out to renew current systems urgently and this eventually compromised the collaborative strategy, which was indeed abandoned in its then form.

Considering the nature of project level ambiguity, Morgan reminds us that unexpected events are dangerous because their impact cannot be anticipated, and because there may be no experience in the organization to treat and recover from the impact they have, although unexpected events can lead to opportunities so improvising can lead to a better way of reaching the goals. On the other hand, the tension resulting from ambiguity can be creative, promoting flexibility and agility. Ambiguity that is unresolved does damage implementation and can cause loss of confidence; so it is a two-edged sword.

In Morgan's view, provided management has the confidence of staff and has banked some positive feelings, they can promote ambiguity to retain flexibility. Nevertheless, there is a limit to the withdrawals that can be made from that confidence, and once people believe management is indecisive, trouble lies ahead. In contrast, unexpected events regularly cause trouble. Management often must improvise and ride the charge that they did not anticipate (as of course they should have). In addition, taking the quick way out may not work for the long term. Sticking plaster may be essential but a full view of the event's impact and undertaking actions with the 'best' long-term effects is the only way to minimize risk to the implementation. If ambiguity or the unexpected event compromises the strategy, the resolution is simpler to see. Abandon or at least rethink the strategy, if you have the courage to do it. Also, see the chance to improve things because of the unexpected. Take opportunities. The statements of the strategy should help turn unplanned events into opportunities to further the strategy.

Another important view on dealing with ambiguity comes from the Office of Program Manager, Saudi Arabian National Guard placing this topic into a competitive context:

> There is an advantage to ambiguity. If we step back and observe those who are skilled in dealing with ambiguity, we realize that they listen to the subtleties in expression and interpret them in the light of their own point of view. There is a real danger in attempting to bring a premature halt to the meeting or in trying to reach a quick decision. Frequently, extra time and effort is required to bring a problem into focus and clarify the various points of view. Ambiguity may mean that business takes longer to transact, but the extra time means that everyone is heard out and there is the opportunity for each point of view to be reconciled.[62]

Managing expectations and perceptions are an essential skill when operating in an ambiguous environment. Ambiguity requires concessions on tactical actions and alterations in strategic objectives due the inconsistencies of market/customer behaviour. However, dealing with ambiguity is an opportunity for consensus building across the firm, because it is a process, which mediates two operating states of now and in the future. The process used to manage ambiguity is first to acquire as much information on a specific issue as possible, next prioritizing the issues for discussion across the firm, third to package issues into logical units or solvable components and finally to integrate each component on to the strategic agenda. Individuals often link ambiguity with chaos and indecision simply because within most organizations there is no formalized method for processing the inconsistencies of market/customer behaviour.

Individuals, organizations and corporate entities prefer consistency and predictability in their approach to markets and in the delivery of products or services. However, as business becomes increasing global it experiences higher levels of ambiguity in market and customer behaviour. Organizations with transnational workforces and customers that span geographies realize that inflexibility, rigidity and to some extent standardization can be counterproductive and can render a product non-competitive in distant markets. Organizations that are pragmatic and solely result-orientated are more likely to fail as worldwide customers engage in negotiations that may seem confrontational.

Dealing with ambiguity in a competitive global environment demands that senior managers play a pivotal role in broadcasting the strategic intentions of the firm to everyone. Senior managers who are an instrumental resource to business units are on the front lines implementing strategic initiatives by their execution of tactical actions in conjunction with maintaining acceptable levels of uninterrupted customer fulfilment. Managers at all levels must strive to reduce internal ambiguities by providing clear definitions of terms, plans, goals and objectives as soon as a misinterpretation occurs, or better still a proactive approach may reduce intercompany confusion altogether. When strategies are crafted and their meanings clear, the organization begins a process of executing a series of tactical activities designed to support the strategic objectives under a set of guidelines that are indicative of the established measures. It is to this process of tactical execution that we now turn.

4
Moving the Strategic Agenda into Actionable Initiatives

In Chapter 1 of this book, we discussed the process of strategic planning and the role of the individual. The dialogue in Chapter 2 examined the methods available to develop strategic thinking within an organization from small venture to large transnational corporations. The essence of this chapter is to combine these two concepts into a variety of approaches to make the new strategy process a reality, simply by making it actionable. Many individuals become frustrated by the topic of action and strategy; this is especially true when just after attending a seminar on the subject they find themselves at the office on the following day unable to apply the principles of strategy within their organization. This raises important questions on how an organization gets started developing a process for strategy? What are the means to implement it? How to establish measures to understand its effectivity? Corporations large and small must create a strategic action agenda which simply ranks and rates the strategic intentions of their business units relative to the goals and objectives of the total corporation.

The concept of strategy and its development has been argued and criticized by academics and business consultants with increasing frequency and intensity since the publication of Michael Porter's book, *Competitive Strategy: Techniques for Analyzing Industries and Competitors* in 1980. Hammond argues quite convincingly that Porter's ideas have often been adopted uncritically (and, perhaps misunderstood) by business leaders throughout the world.[63]

The traditional approach was to develop strategies such as product, brand, manufacturing, competitive, eCommerce and other specific types of strategic initiatives at the management level and hand them down from corporate planning to the operating departments, who in turn interpreted the intentions and subsequently assigned resources to perform tasks. However, now that strategies must be far more dynamic in sensitivity to change and more frequent in their application, the process to create and execute them is limited only by the organization's ability to adopt and adapt to modifications in the competitive environment. Therefore, a new strategy process that is stimulated by a host of factors must employ the combined knowledge of the firm to set in motion periodic strategic initiatives. One could argue that if indeed strategy development and execution is a business process in its own right these initiatives should be regularly occurring events, or at least should happen at predetermined intervals regulated by the firm's synthesis of competitive or market information.

Day describes a key trend that strategic initiatives are migrating from broad 'covering' strategies to 'tailored' strategies that adapt to the needs of a specific line of business or address the requirements of a distinct market segment.[64] Building on Day's view, the need to develop more adaptive strategies is due to four rising conditions: fragmentation of the market, customers seeking greater product diversity, increasing specialization of corporate core competencies and advanced technologies enabling more economical or lower cost product offerings. Jones points out that many companies have internal problems defining the line between a strategic plan and tactical plans. 'One person's tactical plan is another person's strategic initiative.' In Jones's view, it is the role of senior management to guide the business managers in understanding and interpreting the aspects of strategy and tactics as illustrated in Figure 4.1.

Therefore, one could argue that strategy and tactics are two sides of the same coin and have equal value, but must be placed into the

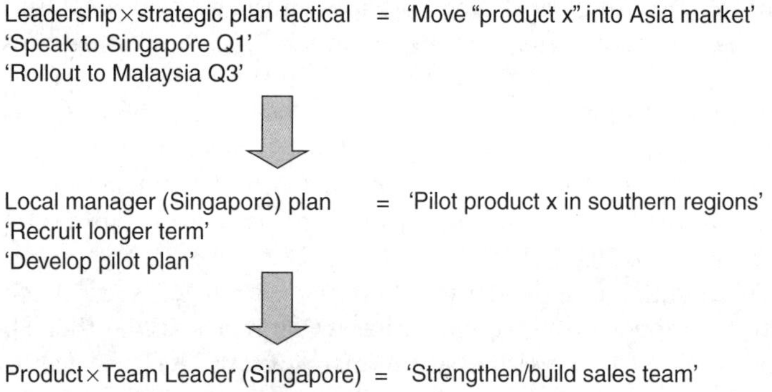

Leadership × strategic plan tactical   = 'Move "product x" into Asia market'
'Speak to Singapore Q1'
'Rollout to Malaysia Q3'

Local manager (Singapore) plan   = 'Pilot product x in southern regions'
'Recruit longer term'
'Develop pilot plan'

Product × Team Leader (Singapore) = 'Strengthen/build sales team'

Figure 4.1 Aspects of strategy and tactics

perspective of goals and objectives within the operating line of business differently than at the integrated corporate level. Effectiveness of a strategy as it moves into an actionable set of activities is directly proportional to the competencies, capabilities and combined skills of the organization amplified by the rate and quality of communications within the firm. Organizations, regardless of size, must have the capacity to execute multiple strategic initiatives simultaneously. In many cases, the people within the firm will find themselves starting one initiative while at the same time executing another and possibly bring a third older strategy to its conclusion. It can be extremely helpful to people who are faced with this dilemma to embrace a fundamental understanding of the types of strategies and how they can be different in their execution. Mintzberg makes a critical point by providing five distinct definitions describing the intention of strategic initiatives:

- *plan*: consciously intended course of action, a guideline (or set of guidelines to deal with a situation),
- *ploy*: a specific manoeuvre intended to outwit an opponent or competitor,
- *pattern*: a pattern in a stream of actions (Henry Ford offered model-T cars in all colours as long as they were black),
- *position*: a means of locating an organization in a specified environment such as serving a market niche,
- *perspective*: a chosen position which becomes an ingrained way of perceiving the world such as when an organization like IBM, Hewlett-Packard or McDonalds builds a culture around an ideology of engineering or service.[65]

Establishing multiple perspectives is essential when addressing the increasing complexities found in today's organizations. New organizational structures, outsourcing and the rise in the use of partnerships, affiliations, joint ventures and associations create new levels of complexity. Unlike in merger and acquisitions, the vast majority of the resources, which control the outcome of a trans-organizational business process, are not owned by the company, but are merely controlled via contractual obligations. Porter makes a key observation when considering the complexity of executing multiple strategies simultaneously, such as the case of Southwest Airlines, whose success is based on strategy that ties together many concurrent initiatives and experiments in onboard service, gate service and ticketing mechanisms.[66] In the case of Southwest, the complexities of implementing strategic initiatives that are interconnected across the organization and in some cases share a common technological infrastructure are reduced by breaking the initiatives down into smaller components, thereby limiting potential interruptions in services to their customers.

Moving from strategy to action is further complicated by other complex forces, such as organizational change at work within the organization. Hafsi notes: 'Complexity dramatically changes managers' ability to understand the whole and draws them irresistibly toward insignificant details and away from the broad picture.'[67] This may explain why in many organizations when strategies appear to falter or become difficult to quantify in terms of their benefits there is a rush towards taking tactical actions to yield purely tangible or measurable results.

Moving into action does not have to be a hard, complex and arduous task; sometimes the elements are already in place and they require a simple periodic re-prioritization. At a New York City investment bank, for example the new director of technology services and information was faced with a problem: arriving at his new job he found that the IT organization had almost 200 projects underway, 90 people on staff and a number of contractors who had not actually delivered any significant systems in several years. More importantly, the business users were making an increasing number of complaints to management on the ineffectiveness of the IT department, making its lack of performance the central argument for outsourcing the entire operation to a third party. The director needed a mechanism to put forth quickly a strategy to address the concerns of the business users while radically altering the performance of the technology group. Having a very limited budget, his solution was to hold an event inviting everyone in the technology department and a large contingent of business unit personnel to tackle the problem. As each invited guest entered the event they were handed two items: a printed programme resembling a horse racing form which listed each IT project underway, and a short, three-line synopsis of the project's goals, objectives and benefits. Each participant was also given ten plastic poker chips. In the middle of the conference room was a large table covered with a sheet of green felt marked off to resemble a roulette table with numbers corresponding to the 200 projects. During the course of the morning, the attendees were treated to short, five-minute briefings on many of the projects starting with the most costly and proceeding down the list. The attendees could place one or all of their poker chips on the projects of their choice. By noon, there were only 16 projects. Any project that did not receive a chip had two weeks to generate sufficient interest in the user and/or technology community to continue.

The process the director used thus provided a means for both the business users and technology group to express their understanding of the values and benefits for each project relative to the current objectives of the organization. In a post-mortem of the projects that did not receive votes, it was discovered that the goals and benefits of a large majority of the projects represented the desires of the business units two years in the past and were no longer valid. In several isolated cases, the project sponsors had left the firm and no one realized that the projects were continuing without funding. In one case, the project to deliver a custom component of software to a specific group of users discovered that the users had been jettisoned when the business unit was sold to a rival firm.

Moving into action in almost any corporation is fraught with problems because of the organization's structure, attitude, skills, frequency of communications and a plethora of additional factors. Shifting strategic intentions into tactical activities requires that companies periodically change their approach to implementation from a traditional 'big bang' methodology in which all things must be achieved in a single decisive step to a process of change that is anticipated by the organization at regular intervals.[68]

Moving strategic thinking into tangible tactical actions

Axiom: Strategies become tactical when visions, goals, objectives and approaches become personal.

Corporate strategies often fail when the organization moves from strategic thinking into tangible tactical action because they often consider strategic initiatives as a one-time thing, rather than as a continuous process of change. In fact, one could argue that the only true constant in business is change. The second area in which companies experience problems during this transition is in the assignment of resources and deterioration in commitment to see the strategic initiative through its incorporation into the new operating state of the business. Sometimes the question is where to start, and at what point in the business process does it make the most sense and pose the lowest threat of interruption in the service of existing customers. When considering the question of how an organization gets started, implements and measures the birth of strategic awareness and the development of an action agenda, Abuel-Ealeh remarks: 'Would you ever plan a holiday – research flights, work out the transport to the airport, select the accommodation, choose the excursions, explore the possibilities of hiring a car – then not book it? Well of course. You cannot always afford to pay for the luxury holiday in the Maldives, when do you have time to go exploring the islands of Thailand? They are nice ideas, but at the end of the day it's just a bit of wishful thinking, right?'

Abuel-Ealeh makes a good point: developing a holiday is indeed a similar process to that of moving from strategy to action; planning a holiday now has many more options than it had a few years ago. An individual can optimize his/her time by using technologies like last-minute.com, which costs an individual (or their employer) little more than time. Strategic planning, especially if it involves consultants, facilitators and the entire workforce – costs the organization time, money and serious emotional investment. Consequently, Abuel-Ealeh asks why is it that action plans are rarely developed with the same fervour and commitment as strategy is.

A tangible, practical action plan can be, and is in most cases, viewed as entirely separate to the strategic planning process. Taking into account the huge investment organizations can make in developing a strategy, it seems contrary to logic and sense that strategic practitioners (internal and external) do not communicate that the importance of an action plan is equal to that of the strategy in the first place. In typical corporations, the development of a strategy is often initiated with a sense of urgency. Companies make it clear that this work is important because they often set the event apart from the organization at a retreat or offsite location, employ unusual facilitation techniques and commit a significant amount of senior management time. However, once the strategy is formulated the developments of the tactical actions are often, after this process, expected to be done in the course of the normal working day.

Therefore, in Abuel-Ealeh's view, the very first step to moving strategic thinking into tangible actions is to make it clear to those involved that developing an action plan is integral to the process. It seems a basic point to make, but particularly for Small to Medium-sized Enterprises (SMEs) or any organization that does not have a dedicated strategic planning team (or access to consultants), it is key to point out that tactical actions are an integral part of strategy, not simply the less sexy bit that happens next. So, other than setting deadlines and penalties, how do you go about creating a relevant, practical action plan?

When working collaboratively to develop the organizational strategy, the initial points that are usually raised will be those that the team can easily identify and, importantly, identify with. According to

Abuel-Ealeh, inevitably, these points will deal with practical issues such as long delays on automated telephone answering systems, invoices not being paid on time, and other front line immediate problems. In a responsive environment, suggested changes to improve the workings of the organization may well be heard and assigned an action, but this is where the input tends to stop. The implementation team, which is often the front-line management, never gets round the entire obstacle course – perhaps due to time restrictions or preconceptions on the part of the workforce concerning the objectives of strategic planning, combined with unwillingness from the leaders of the organization to persevere with explaining the process. According to Porter: 'The challenge of developing or re-establishing a clear strategy is often primarily an organizational one and depends on leadership.'[69] However, we still have the desire for strategic thinking, and the willingness of the contributors to explore practical solutions. How do we get the two to match up?

In the same way as a successful collaborative strategic process needs to be managed and driven by its leadership, the process through which an action plan is developed needs to be as equally directed. As Abuel-Ealeh argued above, any strategic plan needs to incorporate action points, so that tangible actions are simply considered the 'final' stage of the planning process – not the bit tacked onto the end. This gives ownership – thus responsibility – of the action plan to the whole workforce. It falls to those driving the process to present action as integral to strategy. Expanding on Abuel-Ealeh, Bradley believes that the challenge of translating strategic thought into tangible actions is a function of the need for communication of the strategy from the few to the many. Although the strategic intent may well be perfectly understood at the top of the organizational hierarchy, it is a far from simple task to communicate it to the staff in such a way as to generate real understanding, and influence behaviours accordingly.

In Bradley's view, another challenge, once the strategy has been determined, is to ensure that its implications are understood and translated into operational targets and change plans. Making clear the rationale and causality of the strategic effort can be of significant importance: without it, the business has little opportunity to be engaged with the intent of the senior executive, and any subsequent effort to create that understanding will meet with predictable resistance. Nevertheless, even if the first challenge of communication has been overcome, and the strategy is understood further down the organization, the challenge of translation into action remains. Moreover, for both challenges, as ever more staff are involved in the consequence of the strategic determination, the rumour effect grows, and clarity can become victim to individual internalization of the strategy.

Bradley reminds us that when management creates more fluid or dynamic strategies they do not want to be perceived as managing less or not providing sufficient leadership. Establishing guidelines and operational boundaries that are by design deliberately ambiguous allows staff to interpret the execution of strategy within a set of operational parameters. In addition, the process of strategy development and execution must be an iterative one; formulating a strategy, making it responsive to the views of the business generated at the front line, and changing it accordingly. Bradley makes a critical observation by pointing to the fact that if the staff do not feel they guide the business because of what they do or what they know, their disengagement can weaken internal operations and reduce the quality of the contact with customers and suppliers. It is also important to find a way of taking the experience of tactical actions and using it to inform strategic development.

Bradley illustrates in Figure 4.2 the fundamental process which firms must employ to develop dynamic strategies. Strategies are formed within the firm and subsequently translated into tangible tactical actions. Typically, these actions are instituted by a line of business managers and other individuals within the middle levels of an organization's hierarchy.

Done well, the circle becomes virtuous, and real insight can be driven from the tangible consequences of a well-understood strategic implementation, insight that, in turn, is processed and goes on to inform further strategic variations.

Within this cycle lie other significant challenges. Focusing specifically on the 'Actions enacted' part of the cycle, the challenge arises of how to

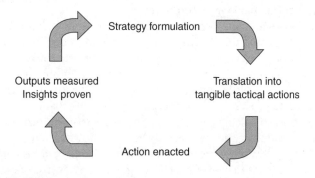

Strategy formulation

Outputs measured
Insights proven

Translation into
tangible tactical actions

Action enacted

Figure 4.2   Strategic actions and information

shape the desired behaviour of the staff, such that their output aligns to the strategic intent. Simply telling the staff what to do can stifle their creativity and awareness of their business environment, an awareness that, by virtue of their working at an operational front line, is very commonly superior to that of the great and good. So not only is the strategic challenge one of capitalizing on the potential of the staff, it is also one of seeking sufficient knowledge of the business to make informed decisions over operational direction. In order to make that part of the cycle effective, the staff need not only to understand, but also to want to understand. Nevertheless, how can the basis of understanding be driven by a desire to learn?

Bradley provides us with an example that both illustrates this cycle and begins to answer the question, one which can be drawn from a change programme implemented in a major UK-based international financial institution. A top-down, strongly led integration following a significant merger had proven highly successful, and the challenge that was addressed by the change programme was of 'unleashing the energy' of the 100 000 plus staff across the bank's business units. By introducing a programme of events based on the GE's Work Out™ interventions, discussed in the section, 'Defining strategy collaboratively', the business attempted to shape staff behaviours, to encourage greater accountability, understanding and ownership of internal processes. Decision-making events allowed relatively junior staff to present mini business plans to senior management and/or directors, and receive on-the-spot yes/no decisions. The process was based on total involvement by staff, from identification of issues, analysis of cause and effect, development and implementation of solutions within a tight timeline and rigorous project management framework. The operational benefits to the business were significant – board level estimates of £55 + million from capacity creation alone in 18 months of activity are on record – but the real benefits lay in what it meant to the staff.

Staff behaviours shifted from passive acceptance of status quo and lack of involvement in shaping the business to an expectation that they would become involved in change going forward. The acquisition of new skills to do this supported this expectation, and the role of middle management shifted accordingly from 'instruct and inform' to 'guide and support'. By going through the events, the staff learned by doing, delivering the benefits while growing individual and collective capability which we discussed in the section, 'Anticipating the competition and understanding market trends'.

Events create an atmosphere of anticipated change when senior managers 'lay down the gauntlet' to staff challenging them to solve on how the business should change. In Bradley's viewpoint, this process does not entail the abrogation of the responsibilities of senior management; far from it – management must participate as decision-makers in an open session quite unlike the normal, opaque environment that the staff had expected. In responding to this challenge, the staff needed to believe that their voice would be heard; and the flip side to this newfound responsibility was that the ownership of implementation lay with them. Therefore, they were given every incentive to develop a breakthrough solution to the business issue articulated in the challenge and by doing so, their desire to understand and solve came to the fore. They began to ask the questions that enabled them to capitalize on their experience and capability. Their understanding was not drilled into them; rather, they drew it in themselves.

Nevertheless, Bradley asks, what of the outcome? How could senior managers ensure that the freedom given to staff did not result in change contrary to strategy? Events were sponsored by senior management, and therefore supported strategic intent. Events thus became an effective way to square the circle of giving staff a broad remit to determine the nature of change, while not diverging from the goals of the strategy. By providing the business with a proven process with established rules of engagement, staff at all levels were able to move outside their comfort zone, learn new skills and build trust and understanding between remote hierarchical levels of the organization.

The benefits of the approach also manifested themselves in the feedback process. The events became 'mirrors' to the organization, and the issues, opportunities and behaviours observed during events reflected the characteristics of business units and of the bank. Individually, these reflections were of immense value to senior management, who could extrapolate findings from the hothouse environment of the GE Work Out event to understand fully the staff in their respective areas. In addition, collectively, recurrent issues and behaviours informed a broader view of the bank. For example, in the retail division of the bank, a pattern of many events was a lack of clarity of the relationship between branches and the operational or back office, in the joint support of personal accounts. The delineation between the two, a crucial strategic issue for the bank, was indistinct for the majority of bank staff, and performance suffered accordingly. By reviewing these findings, the two divisions of retail and back office were able to refine their strategic intent in this area, and reformulate a strategy that had a consequent efficiency improvement for operations.

Accordingly, in Bradley's view, the twin challenges of effectively generating tactical action from strategy (the few to the many), and informing strategy by tactical action (the many to the few), and creating environments for behaviours to naturally emerge are both addressed. The staff become aware of the implication of strategy in their daily working lives, and learn this in a way that encourages them to inform the strategy with their knowledge.

Delineating strategy from tactics

In Leaton-Gray's view, the differentiation between strategy and tactics consumes a vast amount of corporate time, to little effect. However, it is clear that there is a difference between the two concepts. Indeed, it is important to ensure that the corporate strategy is not a construction of a series of tactical manoeuvres. If one defines strategy as getting from A to B, then the decision to go by a car or train and which route to take, clearly becomes tactical. The tactics are important, but the strategy should remain unfettered by them. Figure 4.3 suggests that where it is clear that the action only affects a small part of the company in the short term, then it is a tactic and not a strategy.

Conversely, as Leaton-Gray points out, when an action has an effect on large parts of the company in the long term, it is probably safe to assume that these decisions are strategic. The area between these two sections is rarely clear-cut; however, the decision to define an action as strategic or tactical has no real significance. The reaction of staff towards the instructions involved with authority of 'company strategy' is likely to be different from those deemed tactical. Yet, the transition of too many short-term or low-impact tactics in the strategic plan will undermine its durability.

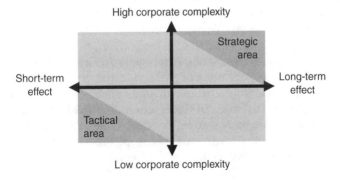

Figure 4.3 Complexity and duration

Ignoring future events

Whitaker offers another scenario, noting that it is impossible to predict accurately future events such as September 11, wildcard strikes, tornadoes or even future technology breakthroughs. However, it is possible to take into account and anticipate future trends based on a projection of when a trend will reach enough critical mass to become a major influencing factor. In many cases, spotting the trend is easy while understanding the timing is more challenging. Sometimes, eagerly anticipated trends stall or lag in achieving an impact on the market such as biotechnology and nanotechnology whose revelations are not fully understood at this point. Fuller identified this lag as the time required to get the population aware of the benefits of a specific technological innovation.[70] Christensen observed that technologies which challenge the status quo often experience a similar lag in adoption because the value of a disruptive technology is often not understood by customers; however, once understood its acceptance accelerates at a substantial rate.[71] Yet, according to Whitaker, the majority of organizations blindly conduct annual strategic planning scenarios as if the future will not influence their organizations. Organizations which do so are able to identify the future marketplace in which they will do business and can reinvent themselves to revive and thrive in the future they envision. The key point that Whitaker makes is that visualizing the future is a continual process and trends of all types must be considered at an increasing periodic rate.

Ignoring stakeholders

Another common misstep that organizations make, in Whitaker's view, is the situation in which executives disappear for two to three days to develop their strategic plans for the next year. By doing so, they often alienate the employees who were not invited, severing communications and creating an aura of secrecy. The posture that suddenly treats employees as spying competitors generates a sense of trepidation throughout the organization often leaving the rest wondering what form of unrealistic goals or seemingly unattainable goals the executives will return with that year. In underperforming divisions, the level of apprehension may be of extremely high, fuelling expectations. The silence leads to more departments closing, people forced to relocate and other life disrupting events. In large and small organizations, it is often true that the organizational consequences of major strategic initiatives are a secondary consideration, in some cases not considered until tactical actions are discussed. In the twenty-first century, people everywhere expect incredible choice, high levels of service and to be treated with respect and consideration, whether employees or customers. Companies must develop a process to gather opinion on strategic issues before they are discussed by the executive team, should be fully involved and measured on the implementation thereof.

In Whitaker's view, most people are told what the new strategic plan is, whom the pre-organization will affect and what the company's new values are. The response is usually resigned acceptance with little emotional buy-in. The challenge for the management during this process of building a strategy and transition to a set of tactical actions is to keep stakeholders involved at every step in the journey and proactively communicate to everyone the progress towards the objectives. Crowley and Domb argue that a contributing factor to the failure many business process re-engineering projects and total quality management programmes is the process of visioning and strategy development did not create a shared vision of the future.[72] Gunneson identifies a fundamental problem of mismanaged expectations that must not be overlooked by companies engaged in these activities. He points out that the objective of the re-engineering approach is to achieve tenfold levels of improvement, whereas total quality management programmes are considered successful if they achieve a 10 per cent incremental improvement.[73] Therefore, dialogue must be a process that sets expectations throughout the company.

Tannahill takes the discussion into the manners through which this process can be transformed into a two-way dialogue, which is a key attribute of any process. Many organizations have a vision and some have a process of translating vision to strategy. As we have already said, the product of the strategy process and its resulting actions will be improved if the strategic thinking is pushed down and worked back up the organization to gain wider staff involvement and ownership. However, an organization requires many of its constituent parts to work harmoniously together if the strategy is to be achieved. This requires cohesion, which is usually brought about by the planning process.

In Tannahill's experience, successful companies adopt a Hoshin[74] planning process to ensure the alignment of the entire organization with the overarching strategy of the business. The Hoshin form of planning converts the strategy of the organization into a series of objectives. A target is then set for each objective together with the main actions required to achieve the target. The circle is completed by identifying how the objectives will be measured, and who will be responsible for

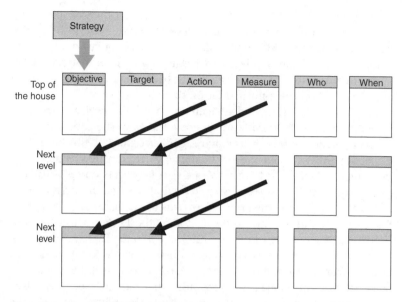

Figure 4.4   The Hoshin Kanri methodology

the completion by a certain date. These are then cascaded down the organization, thereby enabling every level to see how their microcosm of organizational activity is linked to and helps achieve the objectives as illustrated in Figure 4.4.

The Hoshin Kanri methodology contains six fundamental aspects:

- *Organizational focus*: The formulation of a few significant aspirations that are fundamental to the firm's success.
- *Customer commitment*: Creating targets, ranked by customers meeting their needs, setting their expectations to customers and establishing the means to do so at every level in the organization.
- *Focused organizational deployment*: Referred to as the Golden Thread, creates a link between what is important to customers to an understanding of the specific contributions an employee makes.
- *Collective wisdom to develop the plan*: Using a top-down, bottom-up communication and negotiating process called catchball.
- *Tools and techniques*: Management and planning tools (affinity charts, tree diagrams, decision matrices, process-decision programme chart) that is easy to use and understood by everyone.
- *Ongoing evaluation of progress*: Provide a means to aid learning and cultivate continuous improvement of the process.

Whilst Hoshin Kanri is a proven model and process, Tannahill observes that it is also a huge drain on the organization's time resource. Hoshin, therefore, requires complete commitment from leaders to ensure that it happens. This can be evidenced by the leadership team kicking off the process at the top of the house, and devoting time to reinventing and/ or supporting the development of the higher and lower levels of the organization. This process works best when time is set aside for this activity and it is open to anyone who wishes to participate. Tannahill's experience has been that forcing staff, especially more junior staff, to get involved can be counterproductive:

It is better that they learn from their peers that they missed a great opportunity and that they sign up next time voluntarily. The benefit of teamwork and the ability of teams to produce a better end-product than a manager working on his or her own cannot be overestimated.

Process integration

The planning process should also be integrated into the Human Resources processes for individual/personal objectives such as management by objectives (MBOs) so that they are seemingly linked and most independent of each other. A less time-hungry process is to cascade the overarching objectives of the organization down through the organization via the MBO process. However, this is not a participative process, it is more hierarchical and is less effective. In Tannahill's view, an organization has to set time aside for this process to be successful. If this is done, this requires strong leadership. The involvement of the staff at all levels of the business creates a level of understanding of the plan and a commitment to it, which improves the chances of its achievement.

Morgan contends that moving from strategy to implementation exposes new levels of detail that could not have all been seen at the start of strategy development. To illustrate this, Morgan describes strategy as being formulated at an altitude of 30 000 feet because when looking down on the surface of the earth a green field and a bog are hard to distinguish. As strategies move to implementation, the same effect is noted as a plane descends to land in Morgan's words: 'It is only when you arrive near ground level that you realise that things are not quite as simple as they first seemed.'

As strategies become realities, the need for greater clarity is normal; it should not be a surprise to the organization. Therefore, even if there is no clear way of knowing exactly what will happen, some things do come up repeatedly, so they can be anticipated and the means to deal with them can be put in place early on. In Morgan's view, a successful transition from strategy to implementation must be built on a foundation of six key factors: executive commitment, investment, governance, resource balancing, communication and the management of risk.

Executive commitment

Morgan points out that executive commitment plays a pivotal role during this transition from strategic intent to tactical implementation. Successful implementation requires concentration on the job in hand requiring anticipation of issues that are likely to arise later on. While some events cannot be anticipated, others recur frequently and are not difficult to resolve. This is led by the executive board, which owns the strategy and can make it happen.

Investment

Senior managers must ask themselves: how much should the enterprise continue to invest in implementing a strategy? Moreover, while 'investment' is the direct cost of the work the 'opportunity cost' of not doing other equally advantageous work must also be considered. Often the investment is in the cost of changing the way work is done and in shifting the market position at a time when the business wants to send a clear message to suppliers and customers. These decisions cannot be taken once; they have to be reviewed regularly through the life of the programme to ensure that the strategy still provides a reasonable return on the investment. The executives have the experience and knowledge to judge investment in the strategy over other valid investment targets for the enterprise.

Governance

Who truly owns and sponsors the strategy and who can resolve the decisions that must be made along the way; decisions that, if not made, will compromise action and perhaps even bring work to a halt? The executives are the final arbiters of decisions that affect the business. Nevertheless, they may delegate implementation decisions if they prefer to be making decisions that take the whole business into account, not just the strategy. In this event, the board must make clear where the decisions are made and give that person the authority and backing required to make them.

Resource balancing

How should the staff, particularly the senior staff, split their time between the strategy and continuing business operations? Senior staff members are generally needed by both and are essential to both. If this type of decision does not get to an executive, it usually is not resolved satisfactorily, leading to frustration and a less effective use of senior staff time.

Communication

How are the implications of the strategy communicated consistently to stakeholders? The focus of communication should be based on a wide view of the business, one that executives usually possess because of their experience and particular knowledge. If not led by executives, communication may be confused and unfocused.

Risks to the ongoing business

A business often undertakes a programme out of necessity, because the executives see imminent danger or great opportunity. Even in extreme cases, the change may itself carry great risks to the future of the enterprise. Further, the risks also change over time and have to be carefully watched. The executives have been given the ultimate stewardship of the enterprise by investors, and only they can make the risk-taking judgements required.

Case study: retail implementation of Electronic Point of Sale (EPOS)   Morgan relates the story of a retailer engaged in implementing EPOS systems in its 1200 stores as part of a strategy to improve and leapfrog its competitors. The implementation timetable was very tight and the retailer had committed to the improvements by writing the financial benefits into its forecast results, which had been shared with some investors. At the peak pace, EPOS was introduced to 15 stores each week and this peak lasted for almost a year. The risks were anticipated and two prior actions were taken. The first was to define and agree a standard set of actions taken over 12 weeks at each store in introducing EPOS. These were simple and covered staff and customers as well as technology. Without this implementation, it would have been much more difficult and much less predictable. Important though this was, it was the second action that made the difference. The vice president in charge of retail operations decided that, for the 12 weeks to implement EPOS, a regional stores director would be taken out of the line and be directly responsible for the implementation in that region. The deputy would take charge of stores operations in the meantime. This had two beneficial effects – the regional stores director had first-hand knowledge of how EPOS had been introduced and was then later far more able to understand the problems that arose and was much closer to the staff issues than otherwise. Moreover, the deputy took up responsibility for operations thus improving succession planning. In Morgan's view, the EPOS introduction was not without its problems, but it was completed to schedule and required great support from the staff.

Morgan argues that other conditions such as goal misalignment also cause strategic initiatives to fail or succeed, as in the example of a software development company, which triumphantly completed its project early and under budget. The computing system was tested error free and accepted by the client and in a remarkable short time the system was up and running on schedule. Was the delivery of the strategic system a success? It seems the answer must be yes. However, from the perspective of the business unit using the system, this was a failure. Six months after, the system was no longer used, information was not updated and business users had returned to their previous ways. Here, Morgan raises an interesting point: how can the software company think they were successful and at the same time, the business unit considers the project a complete failure. Morgan explains that the answer lies in understanding the motivations of the business unit relative to the strategic intentions of senior management. During the project, conflicting changes were made in other projects and organizational change issues were never addressed, so users had neither the motivation nor proper training to use the new system. As a result, the benefits promised were never achieved. The key point is that from a tactical–technical perspective the project was a success. However, since the management of the transition from strategic initiative to tactical action was not holistically managed as a process of inclusion, education and communication, the failure to align goals across the business blocked the achievement.

Morgan also believes that organizations must do more than embrace a holistic approach to strategy management and implementation issues, senior managers must proactively assess factors such as market timing and the allocation of resources. In another example, a project to implement part of the strategy was completed late because of overcommitted key technical and business resources, and preference was given to other more immediate tactical work. These key resources were not under the control of the project manager. From a project management perspective, this was not a complete success, neither was it a disaster. The project deliverables were all produced with outstanding quality and well within budget. However, from the business perspective the strategy implementation was a complete disaster. The work required to support a new product release, resulted in numerous delays to getting the product to market after their competitor's similar product, resulting in much lower sales and project benefits. Management had incorporated many of these benefits into the financial forecasts for the next accounting period and they were not revised, earnings were below expectations, the stock price dropped and shareholders were furious. In Morgan's view, the misallocation of resource led to a missed market opportunity, and breakdowns in communication delayed issue resolution and adjustment of expectations. Resources should have been diverted from other projects and activities, but the project manager had neither the information to understand the implications of delay nor the power to get resolution. Active management by the executives could have stopped this arising in the first place.

One can be forgiven for not anticipating the unexpected and even for missing the positive and negative effects of ambiguity. However, there is no excuse for being ill prepared for well-known problems, which are often cited as ambiguous or unknown. In many cases, the problems of strategic implementations are known but ignored in favour of addressing tactical issues. Moving from strategy to tactics requires three mutually reinforcing ingredients:

- *Executive-level sponsorship*: responsible for taking the strain as the going gets tough.
- *Clearly defined business goals*: measurable goals for improvements in the business performance demonstrable in the minds of the external stakeholders such as investors, customers and suppliers.
- *Early benefits and value*: implement strategy through a series of releases, each of which realize a business benefit and help to achieve the goals.
- *Risk and impact*: strategy must be formulated on delivery risk and business risk, when conditions change they must be communicated to mitigate the risk of misalignment.

The scope or direction of the strategy may require rapid modifications in response to changing business circumstances. Success transitions from strategic initiatives to tactical actions often depend on the enterprise's ability to learn and change as the implementation progresses. Projects that are the encapsulation of tactical actions may be integrated for efficiency to manage them as one, or because they are aligned so closely that they will more effectively contribute to the business needs when unified than when pursued separately.

Taking Morgan's view on resource management as an Achilles heel in realizing benefits from strategic initiatives, Doyle observes that the issue is further complicated by current trends such as outsourcing. Most companies today view outsourcing as a key in their toolbox of strategic options. Current 'best practice' suggests that an organization should outsource everything other than the part of the business that represents its key value added or core competence. Discourse within the industry is increasingly considering outsourcing core competencies as the next logical step in the trend. Frequently cited advantages of outsourcing include reduced costs, better performance and greater focus for the organization on the execution and development of the core competence.

In Doyle's view, outsourcing activity has grown exponentially in recent years, raising an important question of whether outsourcing may lead organizations into a strategic *faux pas*. One risk is as companies seek to align their entire organization behind long-term strategies, they find that they can no longer adequately influence or control significant parts of their former operations. If business conditions change enough to warrant a complete re-engineering of core business processes resulting in significant modifications to the skills, capabilities and competencies of the organization, can significant cultural change programmes be forced upon outsourcing providers, who themselves are likely to have their own strategic aims and objectives?

The underlying theme to this discussion on achieving a successful transition from strategy to tactics is that measurement plays a pivotal role in providing information for individuals to set expectations, understand trends and market timing, adjust and balance resources, while keeping the process of implementation on aim with its stated goals and objectives. This raises another key question: what must be measured and how often? The next section examines these questions.

Measuring the results

> *Axiom: Results foster measurements while measurements do not guarantee results.*

We are now moving our strategic thinking into tangible tactical actions, but how can we tell where we are going? Michael Emmerson asks a fundamental question: once we have started, how can we tell where we are? If the strategic plan is to succeed, the activities initiated to fulfil the strategic intent needs to be able to demonstrate what has been delivered incrementally. More importantly, the resulting activities need to be able to demonstrate what value or benefit has been realized because of executing the strategy. In order to achieve measurable results according to Emmerson, organizations must first decide on what are the appropriate things to measure. Organizations often fall victim to measuring activities within the firm through the eyes of an accountant vying for purely quantitative financial measures such as prices, volumes, margins and goals like sales targets. Alternatively or in conjunction with financial measures, other organizations embark on programme measurements such as cost benefit, balanced scorecard or employ a business case methodology. However, there is a rising discourse within global businesses to adopt more holistic approaches to measurement. Measurements are only meaningful when they incorporate both quantitative and qualitative process measurements such as the value chain or process performance as the critical thing to measure.

Emmerson notes that different stakeholders will be more concerned with different measures. Typically, the investors/shareholders in the enterprise will want to focus more on the investment goals and so will be more concerned with the financial measures. The executive board, however, will want to concern itself not only with these investment goals, but also with other 'balanced scorecard' type goals. Therefore, the executive management of the corporation will increasingly want to focus on the financial measures and the programme measures. As one moves further into the organization, the focus moves to the programme measures and to the process ones.

Case study: Barclays At Barclays, one of its major Strategic Business Units (SBUs) identified that a significant strategic aim was to shift the objective from being only a client-relationship style organization to being more sales-oriented. Barclays' strategic plan adopted the methodology which focused on small but highly important priorities, or to use the jargon, its 'Big 5' strategic initiatives. The 'Big 5' methodology was cascaded down through the organization, but importantly each subunit, each team and every individual would also need to agree on five key measures for each 'Big 5' strategic goals. These were both quantitative and qualitative. Quantitative measures would be focused in revenue generation as well as activity-based measures such as the number of client contacts in any given period. Qualitative measures must focus on either behavioural indicators associated with a sales-orientated culture or broader contributions to the organization.

In Emmerson's view, the Barclays' strategy was twofold; different measures will be required to satisfy the interests if different shareholders and diverse measures will be required at various levels in an organization. In order to be effective, measures need to be appropriate to their context and so need to be supportive and complimentary to the strategic plan. Qualitative and quantitative measures need to be prioritized and attention given only to those that make significant progress against the strategic plan. Prioritization of measures should mean fewer measures of those critical events or activities, rather than a myriad measures for each set of tasks undertaken in the business.

A strategic plan should give a clear sense of direction for the organization, according to Emmerson, but if it is to add value, it should also set clear strategic aims and objectives. By setting specific and measurable targets, the organization can test whether its stated strategic objectives are being met or not. Therefore, if measures are set to allow the organization to track its progress, then intuitively it follows that the measures need to be appropriate to each strategic business area of the organization. Equally, it follows that measures need to cascade throughout the business at appropriate levels determined by the strategic plan.

Case study: British Petroleum (BP)   Emmerson relates the case of BP that used measures in an effective way to increase revenue from its petrol station business. Traditional bottom line measures of profitability were not used, as they would be meaningless to forecourt staff. Instead, relative measures of profitability were used. The aim was to gain more spend from customers when they filled up their petrol tanks, therefore, forecourt staff had to be able to understand how their contribution would directly affect the profitability of the business. Therefore, measures were developed that made clear the importance of selling the other products in the petrol station. In this way, staff could easily understand that selling 50 Mars Bars, for example, would have the same bottom line impact on the profitability of the petrol station as selling 2000 gallons of petrol.

Managers at all levels in the company must invest in developing an appropriate set of measures that reinforces the strategic aims of the business. The measures regardless of whether they quantify or qualify activities must be easily understood by the people in the business process. Increasingly, organizations such as National Brands in South Africa are developing easily understood measures at factory level to enable 'shop floor' workers to understand readily the impact of costs upon the business. In the case of National Brands, the essential ingredient of their success is that the measures are posted around the factory and regularly updated. The second element is that the measures themselves are periodically reviewed to ascertain if they are indeed still valid. If we agree that business conditions continually change and our business processes must be adapted to alterations in customer and market demands, then the measurements must be periodically questioned. Most importantly, as Emmerson points out, in order to be effective, the measures (like the strategic plan itself) needs to be simple and easy to understand by everyone engaged in the business or supporting the business process. Barclays' advocate keeps to its 'Big 5' rule when measuring strategic aims.

Dembitz uses the Eurotunnel case study to emphasize that the larger the project the more critical the need for everyone to understand the measures. The company has successfully moved from its major project phase (tunnel construction) to being a service provider/transport operator. It has gradually moved its values and has closely aligned its internal measurement system accordingly. Eurotunnel's KPI (Key Performance Indicators) are focused on clearly defined factors directly related to its key values of safety and security, customer service, teamwork, financial performance and its role in society. These are regularly communicated to everyone, from Board down to the newest recruit in a clear and understandable manner. The company has also established close linkages with its other internal systems to ensure that everyone fully understands the relevance and significance of what is being measured.

One fundamental issue is that it is vital that the data collected in the measurement process is accurate. If the organization is using its measures to track its progress against the strategic plan then it needs to be confident that the basic data is accurate. It is equally imperative, therefore, that individuals are appropriately motivated to provide accurate data.

The implications of measurement

Emmerson points out that if measures are to be truly effective, an organization needs to also consider what actions or approaches must be engaged when aims/objectives are not being met. If the strategic plan is to give direction to the organization, the strategy must also address what the organization needs to know, and do when the process shows signs of getting off-course. The strategic plan must state what process for corrective actions should be taken under a scenario in which strategic measures are not being achieved. Some organizations have interpreted this by building into the employee's performance contracts, the precise actions accountable-executives must take when measures were not being achieved.

The implications of measurement within the strategy is clear, if no actions are to be taken when a measure is not being met, then we need to ask the question: why are we measuring this activity at all? When aims/objectives are not being achieved, a strategic plan must have one of two components to be used during the transition to tactical actions:

- A clear set of actions must be defined which can be set into motion when the measurement indicates misalignment.
- A set of guidelines or parameters are established in which the tactical implementation team can adjust to bring the tactical components back on track.

For certain tactical or corrective actions to occur in response to a failure to achieve an aim or objective, data that is collected specifically for that measure must be accurate. Individuals throughout the business process need to be motivated by whatever means appropriate to provide accurate data. The leaders of an organization must celebrate the achievement of a measure or measures at every opportunity.

Care in the use of numbers

Measurement from Parker's perspective is an essential management construct. Without it, there is no ability to assess performance and make changes to ensure that performance is delivering the appropriate results. Measurement is important as it allows us to:

- ensure that we are on track;
- find the areas that are underperforming;
- institute correction procedures for those areas that are failing by:
  - setting up training if appropriate;
  - introducing more staff if required;
  - changing the process if it is faulty;
- remove or reduce processes that are not contributing to the goal.

However, Parker argues that measurement depends on the organization's ability to quantify potentially intangible concepts. It is also important to understand what and why we want to measure. We may need to measure to compare differences between two different approaches, and choose the one that delivers most. Alternatively, we may be looking at raw performance, and looking at how well or badly the plan is delivering. In a number of industries, individuals often raise the complaint 'How can you measure my performance in the multitude of tasks I perform in which some can be directly attributed to the core business process and others only indirectly support the core business process?' Of course, the standard management approach of setting objectives that are reasonable and measurable are time based and those that are under the control of an individual are nice platitudes. Most people can find ways of attributing numbers to concepts, and are able to provide comparative measurements. Nevertheless, Parker reminds us that it is important to take care and ensure that numbers are used in appropriate ways.

As someone leading a team that is delivering customer care, how do I measure the improvement or decay in customer care delivered? It is surprising, but as soon as you ask the question, it would appear that the answer is clear: measure the number of complaints. Does the change in approaches reduce or increase this over time? However, this is not as simple as it sounds. Increasing customer care may mean developing mechanisms to increase the total contact between the firm and the customer, which is good for improving the total relationship. For example, measures are established based on a premise that longer call durations or a higher frequency of calls to and from the customer are viewed as indicators of greater customer problems. When these measures are abstracted, the rising call volumes could be interpreted as an increase in problems, or higher call durations might be misinterpreted as lower quality in resolving problems because resolutions take more time. In this context, the measures fail to consider that the extended duration might be attributed to cross selling or other linked activities within the customer relationship and the greater call frequency might be attributed to customer needing additional information to make a purchase. Therefore, it is important to take into account all factors when taking the measurements to ensure that confounding factors are also considered when analysing the results. Parker provides us with another example, of risk analysis. A firm may be asked how many risks it has identified in certain high-visibility processes. The objective of the exercise is to reduce risk. In the first month, the firm had defined 28 risks. In the second month, they had identified 35 risks. Was this firm now more risky? The answer is no, they were less risky as they had identified eight more risks that they could set up procedures to prevent, rather than falling over the risk when it came up unpredicted.

To demonstrate the need for placing strategic measurements into their proper context, Parker provides an example in the healthcare industry of why numbers need careful interpretation. The European Society of Human Reproduction and Embryology (ESHRE)[75] publishes statistics on the performance of clinics throughout Europe. If one were to accept the statistics, they would suggest that if you wish to have a baby using techniques such as IVF (in vitro fertilization – the 'creation of test tube babies'), you would be better going to Germany to get pregnant, going to France for care and going to England for the birth. Germany has a high pregnancy rate, and England a high delivery rate. Nevertheless, the statistics produce these results because the methodology for obtaining measurements differs from country to country. England measures the onset of pregnancy by a method that produces results later than Germany. This means that the percentage of embryos continuing to delivery is higher in England, as some German embryos would not reach the English standard of measurement of pregnancy, constituting an early miscarriage. What Parker is making clear from this example is that measurement must be consistent within divisions and across divisions and measurement must be comparable. As they say, 'make sure you are comparing apples with apples'.

The objective of looking at methods of measurement is not to imply that it is difficult, nor that it is something to be feared, but to raise the awareness that numbers need to be carefully considered, not taken just at their face value. Measures must be examined carefully to avoid making unsubstantiated assumptions. The examples given above are about context, but there are also examples of scale and strength of measurement. It is important to understand that numbers do not always deliver what they appear to deliver.

Let us take the example of a race; the position in the race does not have any direct relationship to ability. The first person past the post may have completed the race in five minutes, the second in five minutes and two seconds, and the third, twenty minutes. The distance between first and second bears no relationship to the distance between second and third, therefore, it is important to see that numbers that provide 'positional' information do no more than that. The salesperson who is ranked tenth is not half as good as the fifth nor twice as good as the twentieth. When establishing strategic measurements for business process execution one must use caution when interpreting numerical values that deliver or imply rank.

Nevertheless, in Parker's view, there are some measurements that appear to allow comparisons, but which do not. Take, for example, the temperature scale. Something that measures 10 °F or 10 °C is not twice as hot as something that measures 5 °F or 5 °C. Yet the numbers we are discussing appear to be on a scale that would allow us to infer this. Strategic measurements often use numbers that appear to deliver a scale to ensure that the use of these is appropriate to the use made of them.

This is not a numbers game

The aim of assessing strategic results, in Shirreff's opinion, is to communicate internally and externally a true and fair record of what has been achieved. The achievement may not be measurable in terms of a direct impact on revenue, costs, productivity or market share. It may be more a question of how far targets and standards that have been set internally by the organization are reached. For individuals working in a company, there is a psychological comfort in knowing that operations are on course and under control. The sense that (good) things are happening in a company is perhaps intangible, but it is certainly valuable. Communicating the sense that things are moving forwards depends on many things: pep talks, top-down and bottom-up, from people who are in touch with areas that are seeing progress; transparency in everything, except perhaps the few areas that are sensitive competitively. There is also measuring a company against the behaviour of the competition: imitation is the sincerest form of flattery – if competitors start to imitate, that should be taken as an affirmation. If a firm finds itself imitating the competition, however, it is a sign that it needs to rethink its strategy, of course engaging its workforce at all levels.

Measurement is probably the least glamorous part of any strategic plan, according to Leaton-Gray. Using a Biblical analogy, it becomes difficult to imagine Joseph sitting down and rubbing his hand with glee at the prospect of reading the seventh year grain returns from the Upper Nile. He was a strategist; his was the vision that would save Egypt from famine. Yet, despite the way in which your strategy has been devised (and interpreting the CEO's dreams is not recommended in modern business practice), the measurement of the strategy is vital. What is the population, how many grain stores are now full, what are our losses to rats? The vision could not be fulfilled without the information to ensure it had been captured in the reality. However, the requests for information are also unlikely to be popular 'If Mr Multi-coloured Coat didn't keep asking me to fill in these scrolls, and then I might just meet my grain quota'.

Therefore, what measurement is necessary; how often, what detail, what frequency should the information be used by people within the process to take appropriate actions. The effective use of information to support decisions is critical to the success of implementing the strategy. More importantly, measurements are the integral component in the acceptance of the plan amongst the regular members of the company. In Leaton-Gray's outlook, if the measurement demands too much information it is likely that the implementation of a strategic initiative is likely to encounter either active or passive organizational resistance. Active resistance manifests itself by actions such as forms not being filled in, or complaints about the system. Alternatively, passive resistance surfaces as data being sent in late, ignored or even inaccurately filled. Yet, if the firm does not gather enough information on the performance of the strategy, vital signals to keep tactical activities on course may be missed, as we discussed earlier. This delicate balance between the accuracy and relevance of the data and the cost and difficulty of capturing it will need to be judged against the significance of each part of a strategic plan. More importantly, the measurements themselves will need to be revisited as often as any other part of your strategy.

According to Jones, placing the measurement into its proper context is only half the equation; what is most important is that the measurement provides the organization with a mechanism to engage in a conversation on the performance of the strategic implementation. All too often, we are seduced by the illusion of numbers. As a mathematician, Jones notes how easily an organization can be reduced to chasing meaningless numerical measures; organizations consider the following facts: the information that most companies hold is at best, partially out of date, partially incomplete and not what we want to measure. At worst, it is all of the above. Yet, we believe almost any report that comes from a computer as undeniable fact. Most organizations avoid conflict by hiding behind numbers – take the balanced score card, it permits everyone to have their own measure of success providing some organizations with the means to avoid the tough conversation of what is really important to the firm, strategic initiatives such as market growth, cost reduction, new products development, customer satisfaction and other key performance indicators.

To help imbed the strategy into the organization, leadership and operational teams should discuss, debate and establish what key measures must be delivered and to what threshold. Failure of any one of these measures to meet the threshold would signal the team's failure to manage/deliver the business. This is harsh but it focuses the conversation on 'what are the constraints and to what level do we need to perform'. A key question is does the threshold prevent the over delivery in any one area. Jones raises an even more fundamental question: given these constraints, is there a single measure that an organization must maximize to deliver the strategy? Traditionally, individuals have said that their business is too complex to be judged on one measure, although they value the market price of their company's stock price as a single indicator. However, this typically surfaces where there is misalignment in the existing measurement.

Case study: Shell Malaysia Shell's strategy was twofold: to compete by focusing on customer service and to engage in collaborations on non-core aspects of the business. Leadership became a core measure – monitoring the per cent of business shared with national provider and call centre core measure – weighted promises kept with customer. The organization demonstrated three key attributes in the process of developing measures: measurements were embed in the strategy, problems were surfaced quickly to address misalignment of strategy and measurements were simply providing an easily understood and flexible means of demonstrating progress towards the strategy's objectives that the whole company could understand.

Measurement

If a strategy is expressed clearly, according to Morgan, then its objectives can be translated into conditions that show whether the objectives have been met or not. These conditions may be supported by quantitative or qualitative data, but the key is to reduce, and if possible, eliminate ambiguity in the objective (as opposed to living with ambiguity of decisions). When devising a strategy, measurements must be chosen that are pertinent to the business objectives. The measures must be used to support management decisions about the strategy, especially decisions about whether to continue, revise or abandon the strategy. Strategies optimize measurement by finding measures that coincide with data that already exists within the firm and are well suited to be measured against the business objectives. Using existing data makes the measurement easier to understand and more relevant to people during any change in business process. Commonly understood data will be appreciated by everyone, and people will be familiar with the process of collection and analysis. In Morgan's view, there are two primary issues to consider in measuring the effectiveness of strategic initiatives:

● Measurements lead to management decisions about the strategy. The measurements need to be chosen so that they are pertinent to the objectives and support management decisions about the strategy, especially decisions about whether to continue, revise or abandon it.

Morgan notes that he has yet to come across a sensible measurement process that actually supports management decisions outside of those related to financial matters.

- Do not suffer 'death by measurement'; do not make data collection and information analysis bureaucratic or difficult. Measurements are relative to company size and business process complexity and therefore must reflect the business activities that are fundamental to fulfilling the needs of customers.

During the initial flush of enthusiasm when undertaking a measurement programme, the main thing that suffers is scepticism; for Morgan, and a dose of reality is the only remedy. The first point that is often misunderstood by corporations is the effect of multiplication that can quickly be seen by taking the balanced scorecard as an example; suppose there are four measures in each quadrant that are seen as important. It is not difficult to find four measures for finance, process, customer and learning aspects. Then suppose in addition that each objective requires a different view of some of these and that the strategy has six key objectives. If on average, three measures are needed to confirm each objective, in each quadrant of the balanced scorecard we have already decided to collect 4 * 3 * 6, that is 72 measures! The second point is the effort needed to collect and analyse the data. This is particularly evident when collecting data about subjects such as 'learning' and 'customer', and to a lesser extent collecting 'process measures'. Given that the data needs to be collected regularly to check the truth of the claims for the strategy, if the work involved in, for example, a regular customer survey is significant, it will be questioned sooner if not later. Not only that but the effect on the subject also needs to be considered. Taking a regular customer survey, or asking for additional measures of production efficiency, might be novel and exciting the first time through, but it will soon get tedious and (seemingly) unnecessary. At that point, the utility of the data can reduce because its value to the collector reduces. The only way to resolve this is by open and effective communications plus being able to respond to collection and analysis issues. That takes time and effort and so the priority of this effort will be (and should be!) questioned.

Express results as performance targets and measures

In Morgan's view, establishing benefits can be seen solely as an exercise in accountancy, due to two inherent dangers: it reduces the case for change to a restricted and financial view, and it focuses too much on the case for change and not enough on the management of change. Measurements must relate to the benefits or business value expected from the strategy used in context within a framework such as a balanced scorecard that does not focus exclusively on financial measures. For example, a benefit could derive from a reduction in customer order-to-delivery time by 70 per cent. The performance objective might be '95% of customer order-to-delivery transactions will be complete in three working days, with the other 5% complete in seven working days'; the benefit would be a 'measurable improvement in customer satisfaction'. This can be associated with revenue gain, on the assumptions that the competition does nothing startling and the market remains stable – but it is not necessary to do this as a target for projects to achieve. When expressing objectives in the balanced scorecard, typical questions are 'What must be done differently to achieve the goal?', 'How well must this be done?' and 'How is improvement measured – how will we know when it is achieved?'

Although there are many ways in which to express measurements, Morgan suggests a simple framework in which one or more measures are associated with the result as illustrated in Figure 4.5. Using this framework, for example, a business objective can be expressed as 'Reduce the time to process a customer order to delivery from 15 working days to 3 working days, to be in action by October 2001', which is expressed as an Associated Measure: 'Number/proportion of customer orders that are delivered in (3, 9, or 15) working days'. The result is a strategy that has a set of business objectives that can be expressed in a consistent way to measure the performance during the execution of tactical actions.

Tracking benefits

All organizations need to track the cost of work, the progress against milestones and the benefits that are expected to accrue. Morgan observes

Expressing business objectives	
Do <action>	e.g. improve, change ....
in relation to <area of business>	i.e. x process, function ....
to produce <result>	i.e. new performance level
by <date>	the business' critical date at which the improvement is expected

Figure 4.5 Expressing business objectives

that business critical dates are those that the executive management have specified as being important to the strategy and they should dictate the milestones for the projects. The benefit values are those implied by an improvement in performance. For example, if the time from order to delivery is reduced from 15 to 3 working days, the implied benefit value may be an increase in market share and the implied financial value would then be an increase in revenue. By allocating a date (a business critical date) to this the executives and the implementation teams can both address a common view of the strategy, one that can be tracked in two ways:

- How much has been spent and whether the dates have been (will be) achieved?
- When the results are complete or partly complete, what is the actual improvement judged against what we expected and what effect has that had on benefit or value?

By tracking these, the executives can obtain a view of progress that also allows for feedback into implementation and to the strategy as shown in Figure 4.6.

As maintained by Morgan, tracking is based on knowing how successful the strategy is right now, instead if finding out later on, sometimes too late to avoid wasting time and money. Executive leadership

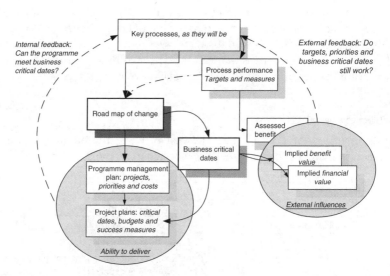

Figure 4.6   Tracking results and feedback
Source: Morgan (jm 992901).

should set the scene by being very clear on the dates they want to achieve results and on the benefits they expect from those results. Executives may even decide to commit the improvements expected to other stakeholders. Whatever executives decide to do and whomever they share their goals and expectations with, they must ask themselves, 'If we meet the goal, what difference will that make to the business?' This question must be asked repeatedly, as work proceeds.

Making strategic thinking contagious

> *Axiom: The process of strategy becomes contagious when inputs are solicited from all stakeholders in the organization.*

In Smith's examination, the idea that strategy can only be conceived and implemented by those with the words strategic or planning in their job title is dated and dangerously limiting for today's business. If strategic perspective can be equated to 'being able to see past the end of your nose' in a business sense then it can be argued that every employee from the post room to the boardroom could at least do with a basic level of strategic agility. Creating a greater awareness for strategic thinking and more importantly contributions to a process, which aggregates strategic insight across the organization, can be achieved, according to Smith using one or both of two approaches, labelled 'tell' and 'sell'.

In a 'tell approach', the business can make employees aware that strategic perspective, forward thinking or an eye for improvement/initiative are important to them. Formally, this can be represented by a capability on job descriptions, a standard objective in personal development plans or even an established competence for assessment against a performance management system. For full effect, this capability or competence must be explained at length and examples of strategic thinking described in order to educate employees at all levels of how they might develop.

The 'sell approach' revolves around communication and incentive. By opening the communication lines between the Executive/prominent strategic thinkers and the rest of the business, strategy can be communicated with real impact – thought invited and suggestions supported. This can be achieved using a variety of levels of enthusiasm and effort, whilst the Chief Executive on a short video might engage some percentage of the workforce, an afternoon in a nearby hotel, with a clear strategic message from senior managers (or even a charismatic actor if necessary!) and free entertainment afterwards is undoubtedly a recipe for success.

In Smith's view, at a senior management level the profile of strategic thinking must be maintained in order to compete with the business critical decisions of every day. Through regular strategic forums or audiences, updates on competitor strategic actions and innovative or insightful strategies evolving in other industries as an engaged interest can be cultivated and provide a vital checkpoint to keep the business as usual activities in context of the overall strategic direction.

Building on Smith's point, Dembitz believes that many firms must make a shift in which traditional measures, incentives and more importantly, corporate attitudes must change to encourage individuals to embrace and develop a strategic mindset as illustrated in Figure 4.7.

As maintained by Dembitz, the attitude of the organization drives its incentives, measures and effectivity of its employees to embrace, practice and operationalize the use of a strategic mindset. Ultimately, the corporation's behaviour is a product of the values acknowledged by the firm's leadership team that trickles down and directly shapes the actions at subordinate levels in the organization. 'Success breeds success' is more than just an axiom; it can be argued that it is a measurable state within the organization, one that is reflected in the corporation's culture. Although difficult to measure quantitatively, it can be understood via the qualitative aspects of the organization such as the feeling

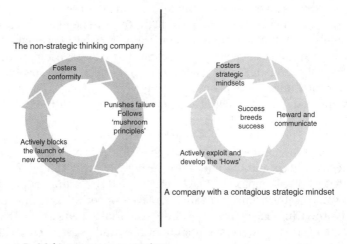

Figure 4.7   Making strategy contagious

of energy one gets at a start-up firm versus the sense of foreboding one finds in a firm in the midst of continual downsizing.

Grunwald shares with us the example of an oil company in the Far East which decided to implement a performance related pay system. Each division of the company was asked to propose the criteria on which its variable pay was to be based. Grunwald was part of the team that worked with the upstream business, the people who look for oil and gas and get it out of the ground. On what then should their pay be based? Should compensation depend on new oil and gas discoveries? Should compensation be determined by the amount of oil or gas extracted, or should compensation depend on the efficiency of the production, say the cost per barrel? The discussions were excited, passionate, animated, educated and heated. The team was talking about what really mattered to these people. Just imagine what would have happened if an approach was taken in which someone had asked the question 'what should our strategy be?' The individual would have got a polite response, and perhaps had a chat, and everyone would have gone back to his/her everyday jobs as soon as possible. Nevertheless, the two questions – variable pay and strategy – are in reality the same! We were asking, in the guise of a question on pay systems, what is your strategy? Was the strategy to build reserves for the future, to produce as much as possible now or is to cut costs? The strategic thinking had become so contagious that the real problem at this point was how to keep it under control.

Grunwald relates a second example in which he worked for a company where 'strategy' had previously been restricted to an elite team of four people in top management (including himself), which developed three possible ways in which the company's business environment might evolve – three different worlds. The team then asked the senior managers to select a few bright subordinates for the next stage, and the organization quickly found and divided the 21 high-quality people into three teams of seven. Each team was given one of the future worlds and asked to absorb it so that they felt like they were living in it. They were then asked the question: assuming that in the future in which you are now living is indeed going to happen, what should the company do right now? Grunwald relates that the results, in terms of both content and passion, were remarkable. Team members came to his office and thanked him for giving them the chance to take part, for the first time, in strategy development. In addition, the strange thing was that, in many cases, the company needed to be doing the same thing in all three, quite different futures.

When viewing the need to proliferate strategic thinking across the organization, Jones asks if the whole organization is aware that strategic thinking is a good thing, why is it not contagious by default? Evidence of corporations with a motivated workforce aware of the corporate strategies are evident in companies such as *Prêt a Manger* where their strategy awareness is reflected as a passion for business in the 'Passionate about *Prêt!*' facts found on the corporate website.[76] Jones argues that to make strategic thinking contagious throughout the organization, strategic thinking must become woven into the fabric of the business. Strategic thinking must be practised and valued by management and part of the firm's operating philosophy is not simply an attempt by management to brief the whole business on their strategy using various communications mechanism. In Jones's view, some level of strategic thinking must become part of everyone's day-to-day activities. The key is to make the strategy believable, then people will become advocates of the business strategy and fundamentally drive towards the delivery of the strategy. When an organization has embraced strategic thinking as a valued aspect of the working environment it has a very positive impact on any changes associated with the strategy as the organization 'wants' the change.

Making strategic thinking or, more specifically, the adoption of a strategic mindset something contagious is not about hype and internal marketing. For Jones, something will be 'contagious' when it is:

- Simple – because complex, vague or long messages are difficult to spread and are eventually misinterpreted.
- Genuinely exciting to the individual – unless it connects people will not relay the message to others.
- Consistent with the business – avoiding the usual business motherhood, only state 'be the first' if you will be the first – strategies must be followed through and must be consistent with the business leadership actions.

To make strategic thinking contagious within the firm, the evidence suggests that the management must set the tone by engaging the organization in establishing a value on achieving a strategic mindset. This is not to say that individuals within the firm participate in an annual strategy event; strategy must be part of everyday work such as interacting with customers, processing orders, building on the production line and other process-driven activities. Individuals should continuously evaluate their own activities in the context of the corporate strategy: was my service to the customer in line with our strategy and if our service falls short of the customer's expectations how do I proactively trigger a re-evaluation of our strategy.

Grime argues that strategic thinking becomes contagious when the company makes it apparent from the start that such an initiative has the backing from top management. Detailed implementation plans with processes, procedures and metrics need to be thought through before tactical implementations begin. Success criteria must also be clearly defined. Adopting a strategic mindset is to encourage open discussion and debate and to question who, why, how and what is done within the company. The premise behind the strategic mindset is to be able to tap into the knowledge base and experience of the entire company as a resource for strategic planning.

Grime's main point is that individuals must feel that their input is valued and their concerns are acted on in a timely, consistent and pre-determined manner. People throughout the firm must feel that they are part of a continual discovery of solutions to competitive problems and are a source to be used in divining the future of the corporation. Individuals need to see that they have been empowered to say what they think and play a substantial part in addressing the challenges of strategy development, implementation and execution. The implications of doing this are profound as strategic thinking becomes embedded as a valuable input to the business processes of the company; it becomes contagious in the following ways:

- *Happier workforce*: better idea of what is going on.
- *Empowered work force*: allowed to say what they want and that there will be someone listening and have a vote.
- *Questioning work force*: providing a dynamic environment that constantly questions the status quo.
- *Better company structure*: the long-term outcome of the strategic thinking company will be a flatter structure.
- *Collective decision making*: full involvement of the company in decision making providing the whole company 'buy in'.
- *Innovation*: innovation and its development will increase.
- *Motivation*: being involved, successful and being recognized are all good feelings, which are attributable to the strategic company.

Grime makes a key observation noting that when an organization adopts a strategic mindset and everyone within the firm exercises their strategic thinking skills, the result is a reduction or flattening of the hierarchy, because decision making becomes more decentralized forming new connections between competencies throughout the firm and by providing a shorter route for information to reach senior executives. Senior management becomes a tool to operating groups within the firm viewed as experts that provide advice to ensure that any strategic plans are sensible.

In a strategy-focused company, there is a shift from the traditional style of decision making based on a model of command-and-control to another style, which uses checks and balances as a method to ensure the processes and procedures are seen to be fair and reasonable. Thomas asserts that in order to achieve this transformation in the corporate culture to an organization that is strategically aware, management must grow as a generation of strategic thinkers.

Case study: Amtec Medical Limited   Thomas acquaints us with the case of Will McKee, Managing Director of Amtec Medical Limited which manufactures high-tech clinical devices company in Ireland and employs 25 people, who has deliberately set out to create a climate in which every employee has the capability to make a strategic contribution to the business. This depends upon their having:

- Information about the status of the business and the business environment which, in a company this size, the Managing Director can personally provide. Will McKee is a charismatic individual well able to convey the passion behind the business.
- Self-confidence and a sense of personal responsibility borne of the belief that their contribution matters.
- Knowledge of how to progress any ideas of their own and how to call upon appropriate expertise in the company to flesh out their thinking and connect it to company strategy.

Organizationally, it is also essential that there is a well-recognized and robust process to support the upward contribution of innovative thinking. Long experience in the company or professional expertise are not prerequisites. McKee takes the view that even a few weeks of working in any capacity in the company probably makes one expert in that particular function and therefore worth listening to.

Thomas thus notes that from the outset, employees are encouraged and expected to take responsibility for generating ideas for improvement in any aspect of the business. Once the idea is sufficiently clear in their own minds (probably tested out with peers) the individual calls a meeting of those he or she feels can help with further information and expertise to flesh out the idea, evaluate its feasibility and support its further development. The cultural expectation is that those invited to such meetings should give it priority and go.

If the idea is supported the idea-owner retains responsibility for its further development. This includes a costed feasibility study (at an appropriate level), for which there are now plenty of models within the organization, and which will, among other things put the idea in a strategic context (bearing in mind that one person's strategy is another's tactic). This results in the acquisition of more useful strategic skills, which can be immediately applied.

This is a robust and ongoing process in the business, not an occasional and peripheral event and several good ideas are volunteered each year from different levels and across all functions. Early fears about being overwhelmed with 'non-starters' have proved unfounded. Given the degree of responsibility which goes with putting forward ideas, people have every interest in making sure that their idea is workable and consistent with company direction before they 'go public'. They regularly test out ideas informally with peers first.

The benefits of this approach beyond the business usefulness of the ideas themselves are:

- There is a connectedness between the original idea and its implementers.
- The idea-owner develops skills in presenting ideas and, as importantly, in identifying the resources needed to help develop and progress ideas. Personal development in more traditional schemes for encouraging employee involvement tends to stop at the brainwave stage with, perhaps, a slightly paternalistic token invitation to witness a stage of the implementation of successful ideas.
- There is a high level of emotional buy-in to the company.
- Staff have, from an early stage in their career, an exposure to strategic thinking at a level appropriate and relevant to their current work (assuming 'strategic' means future-orientated, multifactorial and inherently complex).
- A generation of committed employees reared on the ability to think strategically and implement is being fostered, contributing to successful succession planning.
- There is a culture of using vertical–diagonal groups to take soundings and assess feasibility. This militates against the common tendency towards exclusively upward referencing in strategic thinking.

Then again, Thomas maintains that this appears to work well in a small business who notes that over time, the culture attracts those who will thrive upon the not inconsiderable challenge of being taken seriously from day 1 and has weeded out those who do not want to the responsibility or who feel it is a threat to their positional power.

How easily would this model transfer to a global organization? The criteria for its local success in any kind of organization are:

- an enabling culture,
- a robust, well-known and accessible process, and
- information and discussion about the strategic context.

All of these have to be ongoing, which means they have to be maintained. One-off events may bring occasional successes but they are as likely as to leave a more damaging trail of disillusionment and contribute nothing to a corporate turnaround. Initiatives such as suggestion schemes, quality improvement groups and so on, inevitably seem to run out of steam if they are peripheral to the mainstream culture. The cogs may turn but the gears do not mesh without a combination of cultural support, processes and individual commitment.

The culture

For Thomas, the essence of the culture is one of respect for the individual's intellectual and professional capability and a genuine belief that everyone's contribution matters. There is a concomitant responsibility, therefore, for the individual to contribute. This is essentially an individual-driven position, which may run counter to some national cultures. Might a team contribution be more acceptable? Either way, the individual needs a group of peers as the first level filter/refiner of ideas and provider of support. It also has to be a perfectly normal behaviour for peers to talk informally about potential improvements/developments in their area of work.

In the absence of local peers, peer groups can be connected electronically. Providing the technology to enable this is a challenge to which the solutions are at least known in principle. Our understanding of the processes by which people get to like, trust and elect to work together is much hazier. In the short term, there may be no substitute for peer groups meeting, at least once. Online biographies, online interest groups and video conferencing are a clumsy substitute but may be better than doing nothing. The BBC is doing some interesting work in this area as part of its management development programme for 7000 managers in the next four to five years.[77]

The process

Presumably, this could be common throughout any global organization, though once again, it may run counter to national cultural expectations. Seemingly, online collaborative working is establishing a culture of its own that is likely to be more Western-influenced (i.e. individualistic in approach) than the local culture may be. The criteria are simple:

- It must be non-intimidating, accessible to all, readily available, non-hierarchical and put into practice initially by an individual or team.
- It must be honoured by all those who are asked to take part.

It may be useful to have a local enabler/facilitator to champion the process and support/mentor those generating the ideas. Resources to help people formulate their ideas and make a case could be common throughout the organization, different language versions apart.

Information

Information plays a pivotal role and must contain the following essential ingredients:

- A short hierarchical distance between staff and whoever conveys updates on current business status and thinking and the passion and values of the organization.
- *Frequency*: Once a year visitation from on high is unlikely to support the required 'connectedness' of self to corporate and, in a fast-moving business, recent changes may overtake last year's thinking or may stimulate imaginative and timely responses from the people they affect.

Contagious or genetic?

Spreading the contagion for strategic thinking is, in Thomas's perspective, like an epidemic, relatively short-lived. The long-term aim must surely be for capability to contribute strategically to become genetically imprinted throughout the organization. This is also true for UK plc, with its crying need for a new generation of leaders/managers to replace the 1.3 million expected to retire by 2006 from a management total of 4 million.[78]

Ensuring this capability means helping young people recognize and build upon the skills and abilities they are already acquiring in employment, in their social and community lives and in part-time employment, which they may regard as purely casual. These have been identified by the Institute of Leadership and Management (ILM) and, most notably by the Council for Excellence in Management and Leadership among others as (not in any order of priority):

- the ability to prioritize,
- the ability to reflect and learn from past experience,
- the ability to motivate and organize others,
- the ability to think conceptually and beyond the immediate,
- the ability to recognize information needs and to identify and access sources of information within their current work context,
- the ability to make informed decisions involving a number of variables.

One of the aims of ILM is to help young people develop these skills and introduce them to the concepts and vocabulary they will need to use them. No less important is to help them develop their perception of themselves as people who can make a positive contribution as leaders in their chosen vocational context and at a variety of levels.

None of this is rocket science. All of these are essential skills for a strategic thinker. What changes as one moves up the organizational hierarchy is the complexity of the decisions to be made, the timescale over which the decisions will apply and the extent to which the outcomes will be delivered by other people rather than personally. Contributing to strategic thinking is not the arcane preserve of the top echelons but as Will McKee would argue, something in which we should be engaged from day 1.

In Thomas's view, the role of the local enabler is to:

- Establish the process and maintain its transparency, ease of access and consistency with company values.
- Encourage throughput of ideas.
- Mentor/support those with ideas to put forward. This may include providing help with making the case, working with the concepts of assessing feasibility/viability at the level required and depending on the size of the organization, brokering introductions to other individuals and networks which can provide professional expertise/ forums for development of ideas. This should not mean that the mentor filters out ideas nor takes over the responsibility for the initiative.
- Ensure that strategic information is being fed throughout the local organization.
- Facilitate dialogue between senior strategic thinkers and local staff.

In the case of people working with dispersed peer/project support groups (sometimes by the distance of continents), mechanisms must be installed to help negotiate any tensions between priority of this work and local and immediate tasks. The experience Thomas has working with dispersed teams in the collaborative development of learning materials across several UK Higher Education institutions suggests that where there are competing demands from the remote project and the immediate task across the desk, the latter always wins, regardless of relative importance of the task. The more attenuated the project is from the mainstream, 'safe' activity of the local unit, the harder it is for it to command a fair share of time commitment, adherence to schedule, access to resources and so on. This is often despite the declared endorsement by senior management of the importance of the project. Clearly, reasonableness has to prevail and the local enabler may have a role as an honest broker.

This begins to sound like the training and development role in any enlightened company. To the extent that personal development in line with corporate aims is integral to this approach, there is a connection. However, training and development is traditionally easily sidelined when the economic going gets tough (though not, surprisingly, in the current economic downturn). On balance, according to Thomas, in order to ensure that this approach is embedded in the local culture, it seems preferable that the local champion has responsibility for a major business function. Such a person is also likely to have credibility that is more inherent with his/her peers in the role of an honest broker. Although the local champion should certainly be one of the 'passionately committed', there are dangers in being the 'lone voice'. The approach needs to be passionately and publicly supported as widely as possible by the most senior manager within the horizons of every member of staff in the local company/unit.

Some notes of caution

Thomas reminds that the result of treating what people know and can do with respect may not result in them contributing beyond what they are doing currently – they may or may not just feel better about themselves. That does not make it any less desirable a thing to do but it does argue against overoptimistic expectations of what it will achieve. Do people who are happy at work (if being respected makes them happy) stay with the organization? There may be a tension between the positive reinforcement any organization can provide in terms of promotion prospects, pay and other opportunities and the ambitions of proactive staff. Is there an optimum level of staff turnover which ensures continuity/succession planning but also brings in new blood at all levels.

How important is it to harness ideas coming up at all levels in the organization to current organizational thinking? (It seemed to be assumed that there was a satisfactory and fruitful marriage to be arranged without too much difficulty between ideas and macro-strategy necessarily determined at the top.) I would argue that imaginative responses are not that predictable. Is it only large, rich and benevolent organizations which can nurture the 'wacky' ideas? Current targets-driven thinking militated against it could imply a boundary or retrenchment from the humanist-inspired 'fruitful respect' concept.

Strategy must be a way of life throughout the organization

Whitaker relates an experience that occurred a few years ago, when he stopped for petrol at a full service station in the United States. The service was amazing. Four attendants or 'gas jockeys' jumped on the car. One attended to the engine fluids, another the petrol, while the fourth vacuumed front and back and cleaned the tires and the front and back windows inside and outside. However, when Whitaker returned to his car, he discovered that he could barely see out. The dirty water used to clean the windows made safe driving impossible. Whitaker then asked the young attendant who had cleaned the windows to sit in the driver's seat and asked him what he could see through the window. 'Not much', was the reply. When Whitaker asked why his boss employed him to clean windows, the attendant thought a while and then said to provide 'clear vision!'

The next time Whitaker called at the gas station, the young attendant told him that he had persuaded his boss to allow him to use the window cleaner which his mother used at home, remarking that until he had been put in the driver's seat, he had never realized what the reason was for cleaning the windows.

Whitaker brings up an issue often overlooked in developing strategic initiatives: the strategy must explain or provide a logical reason to employees on why they need to perform specific functions. The application of strategic intent is different at each level of the hierarchy. Nevertheless, a key role of managers at each level is to explain in words that people can understand what the strategic aspect of their job is. Strategy must be lived year in and year out. It is not an exercise for top management, but a way of life throughout the organization.

Expanding on Whitaker, Perez-Novoa observes that in order to make strategies successful ones, leaders need to be very communicative and positive. A leader has to be very charismatic and be very self-confident that the strategy is going to work out. Moreover, leaders need to transmit in the best way the strategy that they want to implement. There are many ways that this can be achieved. However, always a good strategist starts by delegating work and making employees feel identified not only with the strategy but also with the company's values and corporate culture. It is extremely important that leaders make employees feel that their work or piece of work is of vital importance for customers' satisfaction. Employees need to be valued and feel part of an objective.

Case study: IKEA an international furniture company headquartered in Sweden. The owner, Ingravar, was very dominant, but he managed to achieve a successful company in Sweden and later in other countries in Europe and also the United States. Originally, Igravar's ideas and strategies were only coming from him, very centralized, but when he decided to expand the business to the United States, he found that his strategies were not working. In fact, the type of furniture was not customized for US market segments. Ingravar decided to delegate work and assign projects to employees. This was a very positive change, and, with time, employees gave brilliant ideas about the design and the sales strategy. Although Ingravar was the main leader, he was very close to the employees and tried to share ideas with them. IKEA became a flat organization. Employees became very involved with the company's objectives in transmitting the strategy and in delegating work. A key factor in IKEA's success was allowing employees to perform work from the creation of the furniture to the selling of it. Employees were proud of their work because they were able to sell the product that they had created. In addition, they were trained to be their own sellers. IKEA is a case where strategic thinking was very contagiously spread by the CEO and owner, who believed in their employees' capabilities. He supported them at all times and in all ways.

On the other hand, measuring results is important but it has to be done in a constructive way. Otherwise being 'measured' could be seen as being pressured. Moreover, some employees would feel uncomfortable. Measuring results can be done at many levels: as a corporation, as a unit or division or as an individual. The latter is the most difficult or delicate one. Feedback is extremely important to get the best results from an employee and vice versa. Applying strategies should be done in conjunction with measuring results as a way to achieve optimum results.

Whitaker poses an interesting wrinkle in the discussion of developing a strong link between the boardrooms and the backroom: management techniques, for example, Kaplan and Norton's Balanced Scorecard, provide reasonably effective tools to implement strategy. However, how effective are these methods when your employees are illiterate? What if the majority of the workers do not even understand your language and you have to converse via a translator? How are you going to encourage passionate ongoing commitment to strategy?

Case study: The Tea Factory   Whitaker relates a personal story where in 1992, he was engaged to evaluate the effectiveness of distribution systems of National Brands Limited in South Africa, a dominant supplier of tea, coffee and biscuit industries in that country, comprising companies founded in the nineteenth century. One morning, Whitaker walked into the tea packing plant in Durban. The old warehouse turned factory was immaculately painted and lit. Everything including the floor was scrupulously clean. The entire factory team wore clean white overalls and paper hats. It was in all respects a model food factory. What Whitaker did not expect to see was an almost complete 1940s packing plant bristling with machinery celebrating over half a century of operations – a fact later confirmed by the very proud maintenance supervisor. Noise levels were high and machines were subject to fairly frequent breakdowns or need for adjustment. For a lover of industrial machines it was a working museum. As one would expect, those old machines required several operators, a veritable army of workers. Packing of tea bags into boxes and boxes into cartons also required a bantop and a workshop. Whitaker was bowled over by the deep sounds of Zulu laughter over the clattering of the machinery. However, this was not from people standing around and telling jokes. Far from it. Every single person seemed focused on his/her job, no matter how repetitive; they were working at a very steady pace, with apparent enjoyment. It was different from the sullen employees in factories Whitaker had visited elsewhere in the world.

As Whitaker passed a machine created to pack teabags, he noticed that the operator had stopped his machine because it had split the last 13 teabags after it had filled them with tea. He was busy adjusting his machine when Whitaker asked him, through a translator, if he knew how much stoppage cost him. He walked around his machine, grabbed Whitaker's elbow and without a word guided him to the back of the room. On the wall was a huge white board and on it all the prices of packing materials, various tea blends, labour rates and overheads. He pulled a calculator out of his pocket and told Whitaker exactly how much the spilt tea and the teabags had cost. Then he turned to Whitaker and said 'And the fact I have spent five minutes talking to you has cost us,' (he gestured to the room), he tapped his calculator, 'three rand fifty four!'

Whitaker was amazed and asked him who provided these figures. The supervisor laughed. He said he thought the accountant must be the laziest person in the factory because he never left his office. He said that every Monday morning they had to drag the accountant from his office to put the new figures on the wall! He said proudly 'This is our factory. We are the managers. We decide how it will be done. We decide whether we need to work overtime. We all know what we have despatched each week and also know what orders we have received, so we know what we have to produce.' Whitaker asked him if he could read and write. Sadly, he said 'No, but I have been attending our factory after hours literacy course for six months and can read the names of the different blends on the wall.' This prompted Whitaker to ask him about his understanding of prices, costs and profits. The supervisor replied that everybody understands cash and he had learned how to use calculators when the concept of a cash management system had been explained to him. He told Whitaker proudly that he had also been taught how to budget for his family. Whitaker later learned that without informing management, the entire shift had come in on a Saturday morning to make up for production lost by a boiler breakdown during the week. The previous weekend they had arranged a 'family day' when they brought in their spouses and children to see what daddy does at work. They had taken turns to take their family around the plant. His pride was so evident. Later, Whitaker discovered that everyone at the plant shared the supervisors pride in production, safety and hygiene. Surely, these men enjoyed an incentive scheme but it made up less than 5 per cent of their take home pay packet. The message that came through was 'This is OUR factory' and the workers had taken ownership! In this environment, every strategic objective with respect to production, morale, hygiene and safety had been met and not more than 3 per cent of the team could read or write!

Moving strategy into action requires the full attention of the organization, tools to assist during any transition between one operating state to another, dedicated employees empowered to do their jobs and make decisions and most of all corporate managers that lead by example and promote a core set of values. Just as the operations of the firm must continue to produce products and service customers during the implementation of strategic initiatives and tactical actions, corporate strategies too must maintain a degree of strategic continuity. Porter provides us with a view that on the competitive macro-level of the firm's vision, the responsibility of the management team is to provide a corporate context to all strategies as they develop in the business units: 'Strategic continuity does not imply a static view of competition. A company must continually improve its operational effectiveness and actively try to shift the productivity frontier; at the same time, there needs to be ongoing effort to extend its uniqueness while strengthening the fit among its activities.'[79]

5
Conclusion

This book has been a collection of perspectives on strategic thinking from the vantage point of practitioners who devise, implement and manage strategies from inception to tactical execution. They have discussed the process of strategy development and its transition from a set of often isolated or closed planning tasks performed by an elite group to a more dynamic suite of activities, which engages people and their inherent abilities to think strategically. In the opening years of the twenty-first century we find this transition from traditional strategic planning to the new multi-operational cross-cultural process is by no means complete.

Over time, organizations will continue to refine and modify the process of strategy development adapting to changing desire of individuals within the firm to be more engaged in the long-term future of its operations. Mintzberg once again provides us with the context in which to embrace this change as follows: an organization must aggregate its individual knowledge and understanding of complex phenomenon such as market factors and customer behaviour, acknowledge what they understand clearly and admit what they do not know, before trying to prescribe a solution.[80] One could argue that many companies, stockholders and individuals have recently learned this lesson as a result of the dot-com era in which many business plans were based solely on projected futures states of business ignoring the fundamental concepts of managing discounted cash flows and other basic management techniques.

The key learning is that technologies may change and the pace of business may accelerate but competition is still based on a fundamental understanding of value for money by the customer that must translate to profitability for shareholders.[81] From a strategic point of view, corporations such as Amazon.com have been some of the only companies to survive as the technological fervour waned because they fundamentally rethought their business model and industry. In Amazon's case, the management realized early that the key business was not simply selling books via the Internet; their value was in a fundamental rethinking of distributing product(s) using a new communications medium in conjunction with other avenues of access to customers.

The CEO and the management team are the glue and act as the catalyst for strategic thinking, by creating an environment which places a value on strategy development, a measurement on strategy execution and set the boundaries or guidelines on the process of its continued regeneration. Senior managers are the mentors of the process, following the old adage where you can give a man a fish and he is fed for a day teach a man to fish and he can learn to feed himself. In the role of mentor, a senior manager (or indeed all managers at all levels should have this skill) must move away from the traditional command-and-control role being a control point of approval and make it clear to the organization that his/her role is a consultative resource to be used to set the results of strategy execution into a larger corporate or global context.

People within organizations facing the challenges of adapting to new business conditions, look to authority figures for answers: smart leaders will resist taking the bait. The new leadership disciplines that are required to support the change in strategy development and execution represent a critical shift in business context as described in Figure 5.1.

Classical leadership	New leadership model
• **Leader as head, organization as body** – Intelligence is centralized near those at the top of the organization – or those who advise them	• **Leader as context creator, organization as the vehicle** – Intelligence is decentralized and benefits from collective engagement at the earliest opportunity. Leaders create and hold the context and environment
• **Promise of predictability** – Implementation plans are scripted on the assumption of a reasonable degree of predictability and control during the period of change. Activities are engineered, deterministic, linear and programmatic	• **Recognize the unrecognizable** – Intended results are known, plans developed and the rest is created on-line. Dealing with the unknown, discovery, mistakes are natural acts – but not the norm
• **Assumption of cascading intention** – Once a course of action has been determined, initiatives flow from the top down. It is communicated and rolled out	• **Engage and mobilize** – The earlier the collective talent is engaged in the work (recognizing mutual influence), the greater the chance that the latent potential will be released
• **Very effective when:** • the solution is known • implementation repertoire exists • institutions and the relationships established	• **Very effective when:** • business as usual will not cut it – challenge cannot be met with existing repertoire • new destinations/routes needed – reinvention into something unknown • makes things happen that otherwise would not – innovation

Figure 5.1   The challenges of leadership are different in the new business context

Leaders must migrate away from quick fixes to seek and divergent views when possible before making major decisions. A common assumption in the organization is that leadership represents the top of a pyramid. The misconception centres on the premise that the leader is the head of the business, the organization is the body – information, intelligence and insight is held near those at the top of the business – or with those who advise them. Another misconception is that leaders know the answers – how many leaders do you know that regularly stand up in front of their organization and state that they don't know where the business is going? Today's leaders must continually communicate with the organization directing towards key goals and objectives using a wide pallet of different mechanisms such as strategy papers, videos, speeches, rewards mechanisms, role descriptions, appraisals, cascade briefings, internal newsletters, and a variety of means now available via the Internet. The majority of an organization wants to be led and likes being 'informed' responding negatively when there is a vacuum of communication or direction from leadership.

We have found that there is a common assumption in leadership which organizations should re-examine such as 'the promise of pre-dictability'. The large majority of people believe that a leader provides clarity and stability for others – reassurance in the organization that things are going to get better. Leaders invest a considerable amount of time and effort committing to and promising a stable endpoint – our strategy, our mission. Leaders also 'label' the change as an unnecessary evil to get us to the point of clarity and stability. To provide the organization with a sense of stability leaders generate financial plans that stretch forward one, two, three and even more years. The assumptions on which these plans are based is stability and predictability which we now know is rarely true. Most senior management teams would enjoy leading a business with clear and strong values, coherent and close-knit processes, a well-synchronized operating model and IT that works. Unfortunately, the majority of humans do not like change. Note the top most stressful events in life are to do with massive change (family or friends' death, divorce, changing jobs, moving home).

Another common assumption in leadership is that 'cascading inten-tion means cascading action'. Much of what a leader desires is the achievement of specific goals and objectives that requires the organiza-tion to act. Leaders make enormous efforts to ensure their intentions are clearly communicated or cascaded to the organization. Given the ever-increasing amounts of change, this means that the organization has to interpret and make sense of increasing amounts of information and data. At times, the organization inadvertently issues contradicting cascades of intent – there are typically three to five 'number one' priority activities that conflict within a large organization. Added to this the fact that what gets said is not what is always understood (interpretation) and we have a major challenge in cascading action as opposed to cascading intent.

The role of the adaptive leader is to mobilize others to find a new way forward by communicating the urgency of adaptive challenges and clarifying why traditional solutions won't work. Today's leaders must become resources for the organizations holding stress in check until others come forth with solutions thereby regulating stress within the organization. Leaders assist a community of business professionals in discovering or co-creating a solution that is more likely to be owned and implemented. While an optimized solution can be imposed, it is always at the cost of ownership. Adaptive business strategies are not the result of dictated solutions which deprives people within the organization of a sense of responsibility for their own betterment. Organizations large and small cannot be directed along predetermined path…only disturbed. Leadership in an organization that is moving towards adaptive strategic thinking must develop the ability to disturb and observe, disturb and observe.

The execution of strategy rests on a process of continually making trade-offs to achieve a specific end or a predetermined level of an operating state. Trade-offs are the hard decisions that accompany the execution of strategic initiatives as Porter points out: 'Indeed, one of the most important functions of an explicit, communicated strategy is to guide employees in, making the right choices when trade-offs arise in the course of their individual day-to-day activities.'[82] One of the single most important roles that every member of the senior management team must learn is to become the communicators, teachers and cheerleaders of strategy's process and results. The primary objective for senior managers in the context of strategy development is to ensure that everyone in the firm understands the strategy or simply that each person achieves a level of knowledge or insight on how the firm creates value for customers and how management measures the results of those endeavours.

We are moving into a new era of strategies and tactics in which the process of strategy must become more dynamic in nature, more inclusive in construction and more flexible in execution. However, we must realize that this sweeping vision of strategy will not apply to all companies' equality. Larger corporations use strategic initiatives to guide the direction of the firm towards long-range goals and objectives, where the management team knows the goals that may never be achieved. This is not because of poor performance or inadequate staff, but they realize that the markets and customers they serve will change as time passes. The goals and objectives are markers used to overcome the inertia of the organization's structure and focus resources towards a given direction similar to steering a ship as illustrated in Figure 5.2.

The utilization of strategy by smaller companies is more dynamic in nature unlike their larger corporate counterparts, due to the lesser amount of complexity associated with multidimensional bureaucracies. Smaller firms develop strategies that are more readily accepted by the firm simply because in many cases people must perform multiple functions. The reduced number of people enables smaller firms to eliminate layers of consensus building and replace it with collaboration. In this environment strategies are typically but not exclusively limited by the availability of funding or direct resources.

The process of strategy and its development within the firm, like any organization shaping factor must be adapted to the idiosyncrasies of the company's culture, organizational structure and corporate behaviour. The key to strategy development is to increase the frequency at which the company reviews its strategic intent against its tactical actions. Therefore, the new process of strategy must no longer treat strategic initiatives as events, but as a continuous process of value deliver which is influenced by events and altered by intention.

As we have seen throughout this book, the key to strategic thinking is to develop an understanding and make actionable the fundamental

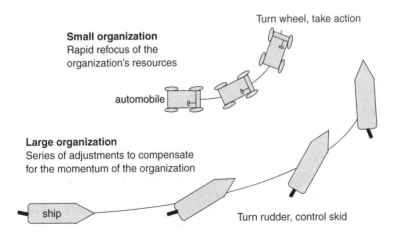

Figure 5.2 Using strategies in large and small firms

concepts that have been discussed in the nine subchapters of this book. At the start of each subchapter there was an axiom that encapsulated the intention of the group's thinking on each subject. These axioms are offered as framework in which to formulate your own corporate agenda for strategy development, execution and measurement:

- The strategic mindset consists of thinking skills that enable the core competency of the firm, which is made relevant by a business context.
- Senior managements are the mentors to people and the understanding of the broader global context of strategic issues.
- Market trends shape corporate objectives while customer behaviour shapes organizational goals and business processes output.
- Anticipating market behaviour and resolving business ambiguities is a process of projecting what is known not predicting what might be.
- Collaboration is a process which fundamentally acts as a relationship with a lifecycle.
- Within ambiguity and uncertainty lay the rudiments of opportunity.
- Strategies become tactical when visions, goals, objectives and approaches become personal.
- Results in foster measurements while measurements do not guarantee results.
- The process of strategy becomes contagious inputs and are solicited from all stakeholders in the organization.

From a corporate perspective, the key learning we have found is that today's strategies must be far more dynamic in that previous generations of strategies, in that they must deliver consistent value in increasingly shorter cycles. This is not simply to eliminate the need for long-term thinking but in the past strategic initiative has developed a sigma of never having the desired effects or are perceived to be obsolete long before their final implementation. In today's competitive environment corporations are under increasing pressure from shareholders meeting the challenges of a growth orientated set of objectives in very volatile economic times. Delivering value is not simply adjusting the duration of projects to be shorter or only engage in strategic initiative that can be accomplished in 90 to 180 days, it is however, a fundamental shift in the strategic planning and execution process itself. In short, strategies must deliver a demonstrated and measurable value each quarter so that management teams can take the progress of an initiative and value it relative to the changing goals and objectives of the firm. Organizationally, individuals must embrace a new strategy process that set a pace at which the organization, in effect, gets used to delivering some tangible value each quarter. One primary observation that was discussed during the event was for many organizations, strategic initiatives often come from top management as a surprise to the people within the firm subsequently viewed as a disruptive process. Since it is impossible for the activities of any corporation to remain static due to the nature of global competition, the changes to the business evoked by strategic initiatives become the most powerful weapon a firm can use to combat competitors. Therefore, strategic initiatives that give birth to actions within the firm that fundamentally change how things are done (e.g. the business processes themselves) are the primary mechanism for senior management teams to use in driving the firm towards new avenues of value generation.

Another key learning was that the technology was not always the answer to business problems at a strategic level. The advance of technology has to some extent generated new challenges for strategic planning and execution because in many organizations three factors occur, strategic technology visioning has become the responsibility of line managers within the lines of business of the firm and no longer the technology people, technology does not bring corporate competencies – people do, and although technology is used as a means to establish a new competitive distinction in the marketplace, its value as a differentiator is often limited to the time which spans each generation of new technology.

One final area of learning, but by no means the least was that the nature of the organization is changing to accommodate the shift in the strategic planning process. The responsibility for strategy is being pushed into lower levels of the organization in an attempt to meld the strategy process into the business to make it a more tangible part of everyone's daily activities. In concert with this change in the process of strategy, senior managers are learning that companies do embrace the new strategy development process where the role of the leader becomes significantly different. Leaders must transition from the role of the approvers of strategies to facilitators to the process of strategy development by mentoring individuals in the best set of skills to have in which to accelerate the strategy development process and helping to hone people's skills.

It was the intention of this book to share with you, the reader, the insights, knowledge and wisdom of the strategy practitioners who participated in the two-day event. Although the book is unable to capture the emotions, dialogue and interactions of the participants, we hope it has recorded their deep understanding of strategy that has been a product of many years of experience at the coalface of strategic implementation. We hope that this book has left you, like the participants in the event, with new ideas on how to engage your firm in better ways to formulate strategies.

A Note on the Strategic Planning Society

The authors would like to acknowledge the contributions from the participants of this event that are members of the Strategic Planning Society in London, United Kingdom. The Strategic Planning Society is an educational charity formed in 1967 to awaken the need for, and understanding of, long-range planning in both the private and public sectors of the economy. The society exists to enhance the skills of long-range planners, exchange and extend the information available to long-range planners and to bridge the gap between long-range planners in industry, government and the academic world.*

The Strategic Planning Society fosters and promotes research and best practice in strategic thought and action. As a source of strategic thinking and practice, the society aims to increase the fulfilment of strategic intentions of organizations by offering continuous learning to its members via events, seminars, publications and specialized programmes. An international source of strategy methods the society is comprised of a large international network of strategy practitioners in many industries. Members benefit from interactions with a wide range of talented practitioners from all organizational levels.

Individuals interested in all aspects of strategy, strategy development, strategic thinking and strategy best practices are encouraged to seek out more information at:

The Strategic Planning Society
Unit LFG 7
The Leathermarket
Weston Street
London
SE1 3ER

Tel: +44 (0) 20 7091 1310
Fax: +44 (0) 20 7091 1319
Internet: http://www.sps.org.uk

* David Hussey, Origins of the Strategic Planning Society, June 2002, available www.sps. org.uk/heritage.htm

Notes

Preface

1. The Four House (Video), Building Industry Association of San Diego, California, available at http://www.biasandiego.org/home.htm, August 2003.

1 Introduction

2. H. Mintzberg, *The Rise and Fall of Strategic Planning*, London: Prentice Hall, 1994, p. 6.
3. Mintzberg, *The Rise and Fall of Strategic Planning*, pp. 67–75.

2 The Strategic Individual

4. *Oxford Advanced Learner's Dictionary*, Oxford: Oxford University Press, p. 1270.
5. J. Quinn, 'The Strategy Concept: Strategies for Change', H. Mintzberg, J. Quinn and S. Ghoshal (eds), *The Process of Strategy*, London: Prentice Hall Europe, 1998, p. 11.
6. A. Gunneson, *Transitioning to Agility: Creating the 21st Century Enterprise*, Reading Massachusetts: Addison-Wesley Publishing, 1997, p. 95.
7. Mission Statement, The Digital Daily, Internal Revenue Service: Department of the Treasury of the United States of America, available at http://www.irs.gov/irs/index.html, July 2003.
8. H. Mintzberg, B. Ahlstrand and J. Lampel, *Strategy Safari: A Guided Tour Through the Wilds of Strategic Management*, The Free Press, 1998.
9. John Ralph, 'Leadership and Ethics in Business, Williamson Community Leadership Program Lecture, Marysville, Australia, 21 February 1988,' available at http://www.leadershipvictoria.org/resources/speeches/speech_ralph 1998.htm, July 2003.
10. Gen. George S. Patton, *War as I Knew it*, London, 1949.
11. Albert Einstein, no reference available.
12. Patrick Dodson, 'Williamson Community Leadership Program Lecture, Marysville, Australia, 11 May 1998,' available at http://www.leadershipvictoria.org/resources/speeches/speech_dodson1998.htm, July 2003.
13. S. Godin, 'Survival is Not Enough', *Fast Company*, Issue 54, January 2002, p. 90, available at http://www.pf.fastcompany.com/magazine/54/survival.html.
14. B. Loton, 'Leadership in Australia, Williamson Community Leadership Presentation Dinner, Marysville, Australia, 12 December 1990,' available at http://www.leadershipvictoria.org/resources/speeches/speech_loton1990.htm, July 2003.
15. http://www.sunion.warwick.ac.uk/uweb/.

16. R. Meredith Belbin, *Team Roles at Work*, Oxford: Butterworth Heinemann, 1993.
17. J. DiVanna, *Synconomy: Adding Value in a World of Continuously Connected Business*, Basingstoke: Palgrave-Macmillan, 2003, p. 20.
18. A. Giddens, *Runaway World: How Globalization is Reshaping our Lives*, London: Profile, 2000, p. 119.
19. Hout, Porter and Rudden, 'How Global Companies Win Out', *Harvard Business Review*, Issue 60, September–October 1982, pp. 98–108.
20. G. Day, *Market Driven Strategy: Process for Creating Value*, New York: The Free Press, 1990, p. 282.
21. M. Porter, 'What is a Strategy?', *Harvard Business Review*, November–December 1996, p. 64.
22. D. Aaker, *Developing Business Strategies*, New York: John Wiley & Sons, 1998, pp. 256–60.
23. Mintzberg, *The Rise and Fall of Strategic Planning*, p. 248.
24. G. Day, 'The Capabilities of Market Driven Organizations', *Journal of Marketing*, Volume 58, October 1994, pp. 37–52.
25. J. B. Howcraft and J. Lavis, *Retail Banking: The New Revolution in Structure and Strategy*, Oxford: Basil Blackwell Ltd, 1986, p. 52.
26. T. Amber and C. Styles, *The Silk Road to International Marketing: Passion and Profit in International Business*, London: Financial Times/Prentice Hall, 2000, p. 47.
27. N. Quintano and D. Reo, *Generic Model for Strategically Managing e-Business*, European Software Institute, ESI-2001-D3/V1.0, November 2001, p. 16.
28. G. Smith, *Managing to Succeed*, Hemel Hampsted: Prentice Hall, 1995, p. 62.
29. J. Anderson and J. Narus, *Business Market Management: Understanding, Creating and Delivering Value*, Prentice Hall, 1999.
30. *Michigan Library Consortium*, available at http://www.mlc.lib.mi.us/about/strategy.php, August 2003.
31. P. LaBarre, 'How Skandia Generates its Future Faster Planning isn't just for CEOs Anymore. Sweden's $7 Billion Insurance Giant lets Three Generations of Executives Set Strategic Targets', *Fast Company*, Issue 6, December 1996–January 1997, p. 58, available at http://www.fastcompany.com/magazine/06/skandia.html.
32. K. Kane, 'Strategy is for the Young at Siemens Nixdorf, Europe's Largest Computer Company, Fast Trackers Mentor Top Management on Technologies and Markets of the Future', *Fast Company*, Issue 2 April–May 1996, p. 26, available at http://www.fastcompany.com/magazine/02/snisec.html.
33. Porter, 'What is a Strategy?', p. 75.

3 Developing the Strategic Corporate Competency

34. Day, *Market Driven Strategy*, p. 57.
35. Quinn, 'The Strategy Concept: Strategies for Change', p. 11.
36. R. Loveridge, 'The Firm as Differentiator and Integrator of Network: Layered Communities of Practice and Discourse', D. Faulkner and M. De Rond (ed.), *Cooperative Strategies: Economics, Business and Organizational Issues*, Oxford: Oxford University Press, 2000, p. 142.

37. E. Chaffee, 'Three Models of Strategy', *Academy of Management Review*, 10(1), 1985, pp. 89–98.
38. M. Hammer, *The Agenda: What Every Business Must do to Dominate the Decade*, London: Random House, 2001, p. 252.
39. C. Fishman, 'How to SMASH Your Strategy', *Fast Company*, Issue 61, August 2002, p. 90, available at http://pf.fastcompany.com/magazine/61/ibm.html, August 2003.
40. IBM's *Autonomic Computing Manifesto*, Armonk – New York: International Business Machines Corporation, 2001, pp. 21–9.
41. K. Hammonds, 'Michael Porter's Big Ideas', *Fast Company*, Issue 44, March 2001, p. 150. available at http://www.fastcompany.com/magazine/44/porter.html, August 2003.
42. M. Porter, H. Takeuchi and M. Sakakibara, *Can Japan Compete?* Basingstoke: Macmillan Press, 2000, p. 82.
43. S. Godin, Survival is Not Enough: Zooming, Evolution, and the Future of Your Company, New York: Free Press, 2002, p. 227.
44. Heckscher-Ohlin factor proportions theory explains the comparative advantage in international trade which is based on differences in factor endowments between countries, Unwin Hyman Dictionary of Economics, Christopher Pass and Bryan Lowes and Leslie Davies, Leicester: Unwin Hyman, 1998, p. 231. When this theory is applied to organizations operating in a network of value the behaviour of market activity can be seen in relative terms to the firm's actions within the marketplace.
45. Edgeworth box is a conceptual device for analysing possible trading relationships between two individuals or countries, using indifference curves, Unwin Hyman Dictionary of Economics, Christopher Pass and Bryan Lowes and Leslie Davies, Leicester: Unwin Hyman, 1998, p. 158. This principle can also be applied to firm's operating within a co-opetition relationship and when companies enter into partnerships with traditional competitors operating in under serviced markets.
46. Jan Stiles, 'Managing Strategic Alliances' Success: Determining the Influencing Factors of Intent within Partnerships', Jens Genefke and Frank McDonald (eds), *Effective Collaborations: Managing the Obstacles to Success*, Basingstoke: Palgrave, 2001, p. 41.
47. B. Nalebuff and A. Brandenburger, *Co-opetition*, New York: Doubleday, 1996.
48. Work-out™ is a trademark of the General Electric Corporation. For more information, see D. Ulrich, S. Kerr and R. Ashkenas, *The GE Work-Out: How to Implement GE's Revolutionary Method for Busting Bureaucracy and Attacking Organizational Problems*, McGraw-Hill Trade, 2002.
49. See M. Treacy and F. Wiersema, *The Disciple of Market Leaders*, London: HarperCollins, 1995.
50. See R. Pascal, *Managing on the Edge: How Successful Companies Use Conflict to Stay Ahead*, London: Viking, 1990.
51. Mintzberg, *The Rise and Fall of Strategic Planning*, p. 321.
52. M. Goold, A. Campbell and M. Alexander, *Corporate Level Strategy: Creating Value in the Multibusiness Company*, Chichester: Wiley, 1994, p. 1.
53. J. Quinn and J. Voyer, 'The Logic of Logical Incrementalism', H. Mintzberg and J. Quinn (eds), *Readings in the Strategy Process*, London: Prentice Hall International, 1998, p. 109.
54. R. Koch, *The Financial Times Guide to Strategy: How to Create and Deliver a Useful Strategy*, London: Prentice Hall, 2000, p. 11.

55. A. Keegan and J. Turner, 'The Management of Innovation in Project-based Firms', *Long Range Planning*, August 2002, 35(4), p. 383.
56. United States Geological Survey, Summary Report of the Workshop on Enhancing Integrated Science, Reston, Virginia, November 1998, available at http://www.usgs.gov/integrated_science/summary.html.
57. Quinn, 'The Strategy Concept: Strategies for Change', p. 11.
58. Lt General Jay W. Kelley, Commander, Air University, *2025*, Maxwell Air Force Base, Alabama: Air University Press Educational Services Directorate College of Aerospace Doctrine, Research, and Education, 1996, p. 11.
59. Deloitte Research, *Managing Amid Uncertainty: New Thinking on How to Win in a Volatile World*, New York: Deloitte Touche Tohmatsu, 2001, pp. 4–12.
60. Jonathan Poe – META Group, Inc., Better Feedback Equals Better Decision Making, *Analyst Corner*, CIO.com, 19 April 2002, available at http://www.cio.com/analyst/041902_meta.html.
61. Depending on some uncertain contingency as, an aleatory contract, *Webster's Revised Unabridged Dictionary*, Springfield, Mass.: C. & G. Merriam Company, 1913 electronic version Plainfield NJ: MICRA Inc., 1998.
62. Major General William H. Riley, Jr, *Leading from Behind: Sometimes the Best Role for an Advisor*, Office of the Program Manager, Saudi Arabian National Guard, available at http://www.opmsang.sppn.af.mil/Newcomer's_Handbook/NOC25a.htm, July 2003.

4 Moving the Strategic Agenda into Actionable Initiatives

63. Keith Hammonds, 'Michael Porter's Big Ideas', *Fast Company*, Issue 44, March 2001, p. 150. available at http://www.fastcompany.com/magazine/44/porter.html, August 2003.
64. Day, *Market Driven Strategy*, p. 195.
65. H. Mintzberg, 'The Strategy Process: Five Ps for Strategy', D. Faulkner and M. De Rond (eds), *Cooperative Strategies: Economics, Business and Organizational Issues*, Oxford: Oxford University Press, 2000, pp. 13–19.
66. Hammonds, 'Michael Porter's Big Ideas', p. 150.
67. Taïeb Hafsi, 'Fundamental Dynamics in Complex Organizational Change: A Longitudinal Inquiry into Hydro-Québec's Management', *Long Range Planning*, October 2001, 34(5), p. 579.
68. Hammer, *The Agenda*, p. 241.
69. Porter, 'What is a Strategy?', p. 77.
70. J. DiVanna, *Thinking Beyond Technology: Creating New Value in Business*, Basingstoke: Palgrave-Macmillan, 2003, p. 19.
71. DiVanna, *Thinking Beyond Technology*, p. 40.
72. M. Cowley and E. Domb, *Beyond Strategic Vision: Effective Corporate Action with Hoshin Planning*, Oxford: Butterworth-Heinemann, 1997, p. 9.
73. Gunneson, *Transitioning to Agility*, p. 49.
74. Hoshin Kanri or Hoshin Planning is also known as management by policy or policy deployment. See Y. Akao (ed.), *Hoshin Kanri: Policy Deployment for Successful TQM*, Productivity Press, 1991, p. 3.
75. *The European Society of Human Reproduction and Embryology*, available at http://www.eshre.com/, August 2003.

76. 'Passion Facts, Prêt a Manger' available at http://www.pret.com/, August 2003.
77. D. Thomas, 'Leadership with Creative Flair', *Edge*, October 2003, 2(3).
78. 'Managers and Leaders: Raising our Game', Council for Excellence in Management and Leadership, 2002.
79. Porter, 'What is a Strategy?', p. 77.

5 Conclusion

80. Mintzberg, *The Rise and Fall of Strategic Planning*, p. 416.
81. Hammonds, 'Michael Porter's Big Ideas', p. 150.
82. Porter *et al.*, *Can Japan Compete?*, p. 90.

Bibliography

D. Aaker, *Developing Business Strategies*, New York: John Wiley & Sons, Inc., 1998.

Y. Akao (ed.), *Hoshin Kanri: Policy Deployment for Successful TQM*, Productivity Press, 1991.

T. Amber and C. Styles, *The Silk Road to International Marketing: Passion and Profit in International Business*, London: Financial Times/Prentice-Hall International, 2000.

J. Anderson and J. Narus, *Business Market Management: Understanding, Creating and Delivering Value*, London: Prentice-Hall International, 1999.

H. Igor Ansoff, 'Synergy and Capabilities', A. Campbell *et al.* (eds), *Strategic Synergy*, London: International Thompson Business Press, 1998.

J. Belasco, *Teaching the Elephant to Dance*, London: Hutchinson Business, 1990.

M. J. Blaine, *Co-operation in International Business*, Aldershot: Avebury, 1994.

R. Camrass and M. Farncombe, *The Atomic Corporation: A Rational Proposal for Uncertain Times*, Oxford: Capstone Publishing, 2001.

E. Chaffee, 'Three Models of Strategy', *Academy of Management Review*, 10(1), 1985.

J. Champy, *X-Engineering the Corporation. Reinvent your Business in the Digital Age*, London: Hodder and Stoughton, 2002.

M. Cowley and E. Domb, *Beyond Strategic Vision: Effective Corporate Action with Hoshin Planning*, Oxford: Butterworth-Heinemann, 1997.

T. Davenport and L. Prusak, *Working Knowledge: How Organizations Manage What They Know*, Boston: Harvard Business School Press, 1998.

W. H. Davidow and M. S. Malone, *The Virtual Corporation. Structuring and Revitalizing the Corporation for the 21st Century*, London: Harper Business, 1993.

S. Davis and B. Davidson, *2020 Vision: Transform your Business Today to Succeed in Tomorrow's Economy*, London: Business Books Ltd, 1991.

G. Day, *Market Driven Strategy: Process for Creating Value*, New York: The Free Press, 1990.

G. Day, 'The Capabilities of Market Driven Organizations', *Journal of Marketing*, 58, October 1994, pp. 37–52.

J. DiVanna, *Thinking Beyond Technology: Creating New Value in Business*, Basingstoke: Palgrave Macmillan, 2003.

J. DiVanna, *Synconomy: Adding Value in a World of Continuously Connected Business*, Basingstoke: Palgrave Macmillan, 2003.

P. Evans and T. Wurster, 'Strategy and the New Economics of Information', D. Tapscott (ed.), *Creating Value in the Network Economy*, Boston: Harvard Business School Press, 1999.

L. Frimanson and J. Lind, 'The Balanced Scorecard and Learning in Business Relationships', H. Hakansson and J. Johanson (eds), *Business Network Learning*, Oxford: Elsevier Science Limited, 2001.

M. Goold, A. Campbell and M. Alexander, *Corporate Level Strategy: Creating Value in the Multibusiness Company*, Chichester: Wiley, 1994.

A. Gunneson, *Transitioning to Agility: Creating the 21st Century Enterprise*, Reading, Massachusetts: Addison-Wesley Publishing, 1997.

M. Hammer, *The Agenda: What Every Business Must do to Dominate the Decade*, London: Random House, 2001.

M. Hammer and J. Champy, *Reengineering the Corporation: A Manifesto for Business Revolution*, London: Nicholas Brealey Publishing, 2001.

C. Handy, 'Trust and the Virtual Organization', D. Tapscott (ed.), *Creating Value in the Network Economy*, Boston: Harvard Business Review Book, 1999.

P. Hines, R. Lamming, D. Jones, P. Cousins and N. Rich, *Value Stream Management: Strategy and Excellence in the Supply Chain*, Harlow: Pearson Education Ltd, 2000.

Hout, Porter and Rudden, 'How Global Companies Win Out', *Harvard Business Review*, Issue 60, September–October 1982.

J. B. Howcraft and J. Lavis, *Retail Banking: The New Revolution in Structure and Strategy*, Oxford: Basil Blackwell Ltd, 1986.

J. C. Jarillo, *Strategic Networks: Creating the Borderless Organization*, Oxford: Butterworth-Heinemann, 1993.

R. Kaplan and D. Norton, *The Strategy Focused Organization*, Boston: Harvard Business School Press, 2001.

A. Keegan and J. Turner, 'The Management of Innovation in Project-Based Firms', *Long Range Planning*, 35(4), August 2002.

R. Koch, *The Financial Times Guide to Strategy: How to Create and Deliver a Useful Strategy*, London: Prentice-Hall International, 2000.

R. Loveridge, 'The Firm as Differentiator and Integrator of Network: Layered Communities of Practice and Discourse', D. Faulkner and M. De Rond (eds), *Cooperative Strategies: Economics, Business and Organizational Issues*, Oxford: Oxford University Press, 2000.

J. Micklethwait and A. Wooldridge, *A Future Perfect*, London: William Heinemann, 2000.

H. Mintzberg, *The Rise and Fall of Strategic Planning*, London: Prentice-Hall International, 1994.

H. Mintzberg, 'The Strategy Process: Five Ps for Strategy', D. Faulkner and M. De Rond (eds), *Cooperative Strategies: Economics, Business and Organizational Issues*, Oxford: Oxford University Press, 2000.

H. Mintzberg, B. Ahlstrand and J. Lampel, *Strategy Safari: A Guided Tour Through the Wilds of Strategic Management*, New York: The Free Press, 1998.

B. Nalebuff and A. Brandenburger, *Co-opetition*, New York: Doubleday, 1996.

R. Pascal, *Managing on the Edge: How Successful Companies Use Conflict to Stay Ahead*, London: Viking, 1990.

Gen. George S. Patton, *War as I Knew it*, London, 1949.

M. Porter, *Competitive Advantage*, New York: The Free Press, 1985.

M. Porter, 'What is a Strategy?', *Harvard Business Review*, November–December 1996.

M. Porter, 'Strategy and the Internet', *Harvard Business Review*, March 2001.

M. Porter, H. Takeuchi and M. Sakakibara, *Can Japan Compete?* Basingstoke: Macmillan Press, 2000.

J. Quinn, 'The Strategy Concept: Strategies for Change', H. Mintzberg, J. Quinn and S. Ghoshal (eds), *The Process of Strategy*, London: Prentice-Hall Europe, 1998.

J. Quinn and J. Voyer, 'The Logic of Logical Incrementallsm', H. Mintzbcrg and J. Quinn (eds), *Readings in the Strategy Process*, London: Prentice-Hall International, 1998.

N. Quintano and D. Reo, *Generic Model for Strategically Managing e-Business*, European Software Institute, ESI-2001-D3/V1.0, November 2001.

G. Smith, *Managing to Succeed*, Hemel Hampsted: Prentice Hall, 1995.

D. Thomas, 'Leadership with Creative Flair', *Edge*, 2(3), October 2003.

M. Treacy and F. Wiersema, *The Discipline of Market Leaders*, Reading, Massachusetts: Perseus Books, 1997.

D. Ulrich, S. Kerr and R. Ashkenas, *The GE Work-Out: How to Implement GE's Revolutionary Method for Busting Bureaucracy and Attacking Organizational Problems*, McGraw-Hill Trade, 2002.

Index